W9-AHN-890

Collaboration Handbook

Creating, Sustaining, and Enjoying the Journey

by Michael Winer and Karen Ray

FIELDSTONE
ALLIANCE

SAINT PAUL
MINNESOTA

We thank the David and Lucile Packard Foundation,
Los Altos, California, for underwriting development of this book.

Copyright © 1994 by Fieldstone Alliance.

Fieldstone Alliance is committed to strengthening the performance of the nonprofit sector. Through the synergy of its consulting, training, publishing, and research and demonstration projects, Fieldstone Alliance provides solutions to issues facing the nonprofit sector. Fieldstone Alliance was formerly a department of the Amherst H. Wilder Foundation. If you would like more information about Fieldstone Alliance and our services, please contact

> Fieldstone Alliance
> 60 Plato Boulevard East, Suite 150
> Saint Paul, MN 55107
> 800-274-6024

We hope you find this book helpful! For more information about other Fieldstone Alliance publications, please see the back of this book or contact:

> Fieldstone Alliance
> 60 Plato Boulevard East, Suite 150
> Saint Paul, MN 55107
>
> 800-274-6024
> www.FieldstoneAlliance.org

Edited by Dee Ready and Vince Hyman
Illustrated by Kate Mueller
Designed by Rebecca Andrews

Manufactured in the United States of America
Ninth printing, October 2007

Library of Congress Cataloging-in-Publication Data

Winer, Michael Barry
    Collaboration handbook : creating, sustaining, and enjoying the journey / by Michael Winer and Karen Ray.
        p.   cm.
    Includes bibliographical references and index.
    ISBN-13: 978-0-940069-03-9
    ISBN-10: 0-940069-03-2
    1. Work groups.   2. Interorganizational relations.
3. Organizational change.   I. Ray, Karen Louise
II. Title.
HD66.W557   1994   94-6139
658.4'02--dc20   CIP

Limited permission to copy

We have developed this publication to benefit nonprofit and community organizations. To enable this, we grant the purchaser of this work limited permission to reproduce worksheets, forms, charts, graphics, or brief excerpts from the book so long as the reproductions are for direct use by the individual or organization that purchased the book and not for use by others outside the organization. For example, an organization that purchased the book to help its staff or board make plans relevant to the topic of this book may make copies of material from the book to distribute to others in the organization as they plan. Some of the worksheets in this book may be available for download from the publisher's web site. The same conditions expressed here apply to the use of downloadable worksheets.

Limits

The worksheets may NOT be reproduced for training outside the organization that purchased the book. For example, a consultant may not purchase one copy of this work and then use the worksheets with multiple organizations. In this case, the organization that the consultant is working with should purchase a copy of the book. Nor may an "umbrella organization" purchase a single copy of the book and then make copies of key worksheets for every member organization under its umbrella.

For permission to make multiple copies outside of the permission granted here—for example, for training, for use in a compilation of materials, for public presentation, or to otherwise distribute portions of the book to organizations and individuals that did not purchase the book—please visit the publisher's web site, **www.FieldstoneAlliance.org/ permissions.**

Aside from the limited permission granted here, all other rights not expressly granted here are reserved.

Printed on recycled paper
10% postconsumer waste

About the Authors

Michael Winer

Michael Winer is the founder of Synoptics: Seeing the Whole Together, which is dedicated to unifying individual and organizational actions that mobilize community-wide efforts and resources to meet the needs of our society. He has worked closely with community members and leaders from all sectors: education, philanthropy, law enforcement, religion, government, business, health care, and human services. With over twenty years of national experience, Michael has been successful at bringing together people of diverse talents and perspectives so they can achieve common visions and take joint actions. Prior to founding Synoptics, Michael was Director of the Community Collaboration Venture for the A. H. Wilder Foundation in Saint Paul, Minnesota. In addition, he taught for four years in Japan and has been a program manager with the United Way. Michael has a Master's Degree in Applied Behavioral Sciences.

Karen Ray

Karen Ray is President of Karen Ray Associates, which specializes in staff training and organizational development. With a Master's Degree in Applied Behavioral Sciences, her work focuses on collaboration, team building, and leadership. Active with Metropolitan State University in Saint Paul, Minnesota, Karen teaches team building and communications courses. Before beginning her practice in 1983, Karen was executive director of a literacy agency. During these years, she developed collaborations to improve services for illiterate adults and modify legislation regarding adult education. ◆

This book is dedicated to Len Hirsch, a great friend and teacher to many.
His work infuses this book. May his memory be for a blessing.

Acknowledgments

Many people helped us along the road. Thanks to Gary Stern for securing the funding that helped underwrite the development costs; to Geri Rivard, the Executive Director, and the Board of Trustees of the Packard Foundation for generously supporting the development of this book; to Dee Ready who gave the book a special zest; and to Becky Andrews and Vince Hyman of Fieldstone Alliance for zealously pursuing excellence.

Paul Mattessich and Barbara Monsey at the Wilder Research Center provided the underpinnings for this book in their report, *Collaboration: What Makes It Work—A Review of Research Literature on Factors Influencing Successful Collaboration*. Thank you.

Special thanks to the staff at the Amherst H. Wilder Foundation and the more than sixty people throughout the country who brought their community and professional experience as well as their cultural, ethnic, and geographic viewpoints to reviewing this book. These reviewers helped ensure that the book works for many people in many places.

Karen says: Many of the concepts in this book were tried and tested by the literacy professionals in Minnesota; thanks to Bob Gramstad for providing leadership. This book would not have been possible without Cynthia Heelan, who puts these practices to work everyday, and without Dave and Max, who believed in me. And, of course, thanks to Nancy Ketchel, whose unswerving regard has proved that friendship is the best collaboration of all.

Michael says: Thank you to the many people who let me work with them around the country. Your struggles and discoveries infuse this book. Deborah Bennet-Leet, Dick Molohon, Shirley Pierce, Grace Tangjerd-Schmitt and Carol Truesdell know that building relationships is the key to success; thank you for my friendship with each of you and for your support. Joan Poritsky provided the impetus to write this book; she helped me learn to first act collaboratively. Anne Graves offered questions and thoughts that led to the framework. Above all, thanks to my wife, Dianne, and daughter, Lael; you gave me the time, space and emotional support to journey down this long road with Karen.

And finally, Karen and Michael thank each other for the incredibly fruitful working relationship with all its creativity and stimulating conflict. This book is our first milestone. ◆

> *No matter where we are on the road, some people are ahead of us and some people are behind us.*
>
> —Lael Winer-Cyr
> 15-year-old student

Contents

Preface

Many problems face us: hunger, homelessness, pollution, budget deficits, urban decay, arts under attack, medical costs and coverage. Violence plagues the country, and prisons have not lowered crime rates. Businesses need to be more competitive while unions struggle with their role. Entry level jobs require critical thinking skills, yet schools are faced with mounting social problems that hinder education. Government demands compliance to a host of separate rules, and foundations fund mostly individual programs for one or two years, leaving them to scramble for additional funds.

All of these problems are interrelated. Thus, we need to address the common sources of the problems rather than waiting to fix separate symptoms. We need to think of long-term changes as well as short-term actions. No one person or group alone can confront our problems for long.

Individually, good people and organizations are agreeing to do something about these problems. But we live in a highly interrelated global society, and actions within a single sector of society affect many other sectors in many other places. And each of these places has its own stakeholders.

Bringing together diverse stakeholders, melding their resources, and stretching their minds to embrace new ideas and a new language is essential to resolving our problems. Is there some way people can work together to resolve these problems over time? Yes. Collaboration provides an opportunity and a challenge to bring people together in ways that are *more than the sum of individuals*. And we can apply many of the key elements of effective collaboration to any joint effort.

Collaboration is a process that gets people to work together in new ways. The process does not end but spawns new collaborative ventures. Collaboration becomes a continuing phenomenon with a wide range of results that empower people and systems to change.

Let's take a closer look at what collaboration is—and is not—and find out how to create, sustain, and enjoy the collaborative journey. ◆

> "
> *We are caught in an inescapable network of mutuality, tied in a single garment of destiny. Whatever affects one directly, affects all indirectly.*
> — *Martin Luther King (1929–1968) American clergyman and civil rights leader*
> "

How to Use This Book

"

The longest part of the journey is said to be the passing of the gate.

— *Marcus Terentius Varro (116–27 BCE) Roman author*

"

Working together provides opportunities to achieve results we are more likely to achieve together than alone. These joint efforts—collaborations—demand relating to one another and working together in innovative ways. This book helps us learn about creating, sustaining, and enjoying new ways of working together.

Collaboration is a journey, and, like many roads, it is full of twists and turns. Because working together can be so complex, this book asks more of us than simply staying between the traffic lines. This book asks us to:

- **Use the language of "we" and "our" and "us."** You and I cannot achieve what *we* can achieve. This book uses language to reinforce a new identity for partners who collaborate.

- **Embrace complexity and ambiguity.** Collaboration is not an easy fix; for instance, it requires more complex long-term thinking and conflict management. Building trust, organizing the effort, evaluating the results, and involving our communities are all part of collaboration. Yet these elements remain ambiguous, requiring continual redefinition.

To help us learn a new language and deal with sometimes complicated situations, this book—our gateway to the journey—is divided into four parts.

PART I offers *a story* to help us see, in action, the stages and challenges of collaboration. This story is referred to throughout this book as a guide to understanding collaboration.

PART II supplies a *definition of collaboration* and applies the *metaphor of journey* to the process of collaboration. This definition and metaphor provide a framework for the rest of the book.

PART III details the *four stages of collaboration* and their respective challenges, described geographically to remind us of where we are in the journey. This part supplies the step-by-step "how to" guide to our journey. Part III also provides additional ideas as:

Go Slow Signs—important items to note in making collaborations work well. (For a complete list of these, look under "Go Slow Signs" in the index.)

 Guide Books—enriched information about a particular aspect of the journey. (For a complete list of these, look under "Guide Books" in the index.)

 Milestones—brief summaries that let us know when we've finished a leg of the journey.

PART IV contains *appendices*—the research base for collaboration; a resource section of books and articles; and forms for documenting the collaboration. The forms correspond to each of the challenges described in Part III and are meant to be used as each challenge is met.

To best meet their individual needs and extract the most from this book, readers—travelers—should move around the book as they choose. For example, travelers who prefer an itinerary—a step-by-step description of what to do—might read **Part III** first; it describes the four stages of collaboration sequentially. Travelers who have had experience with collaboration and know that this journey is not a straight route might search the **Contents** and **Index** like maps for specific information and go directly to their destination. Travelers who learn best from example may prefer the story in **Part I**, which gives a quick overview of the people and problems that collaboration partners often encounter. Travelers who want only the big picture can go immediately to **Part II,** which gives the framework for working together. Highly experienced travelers may need only the worksheets in **Part IV**.

However it is used, the *Collaboration Handbook* can help start any kind of joint effort, improve an existing collaboration, or help test the waters with a small project.

◆ ◆ ◆

Collaboration has become the new buzz word! People use it to describe any time they get together for a purpose beyond normal duties or interests. True collaboration means doing things very differently than we've done them before. This book looks at the relationships we need to build and the work we need to do to make our collaboration successful.

Each collaboration is unique. Can a generic book help with specific needs? YES! The definition, metaphor, and detailed steps in the four stages provide a model that helps members create, sustain, and enjoy their collaborative journey. ◆

> **"**
> *A mind stretched by a new idea will never return to its original position.*
> — *Don Coyhis*
> *Founder,*
> *White Bison, Inc.*
> **"**

How Do We Begin?

Let's Share a Story

How Do We Begin?

Let's Share a Story

As we begin our journey together, we first meet a group of people who accepted the challenge of joining in a collaborative effort. Their story invites us to consider two aspects of collaboration: *what it offers* and *what it demands*.

The experiences of the characters in this story help us appreciate the theory-in-action behind the four stages and the challenges we will encounter as we study the challenges of collaboration in Part III. The story provides a touchstone for our understanding of the remainder of this book.

One note before beginning: the narration follows the four stages and their key challenges that Part III of this book explores. The margin notes refer to the appropriate challenge and page in Part III. To explore an intriguing aspect of the challenge, simply turn to the page given in bold in the margin, spend some time there, and then return to the story.

Note that some of the challenges are not in the sequence described in Part III of this book. This is because collaborations are made up of real people who do not conform to research. For example, while conflict is explored in Stage 2 of the journey, real people may experience conflict in any of the four stages. Similarly, disclosing self-interests, while important in Stage 1, may occur at anytime. This reminds us that the road on our journey is not straight, but twists and turns.

Enough said. The story awaits us.

> "
> *Even the seasons form a great circle in their changing, and always come back to where they were.*
>
> — *Black Elk*
> *Holy man of the Oglala Sioux*
> "

The Scene

Setting

The collaboration members in this story work together for almost two years in a semirural part of the state that includes:

- GREEN VALLEY, a town of 12,000 clustered around factories owned by Good Foods, Inc. These factories freeze and can vegetables grown in the surrounding area.

- ROCKVILLE, an education center of 43,000 (not counting students) with a regional high school, technical college, and a state university as its main employers.

- METFORD, a county seat of 97,000 residents employed primarily in industries related to agriculture, county government, and health care.

Need

Farm laborers, migrants, young people, and now families are increasingly homeless. They may also need drug treatment, health care, mental health services, and access to government programs such as Aid to Families with Dependent Children (AFDC).

Key Players

In Green Valley:

The Tri-County Community Improvement Project
Betty Jackson, Executive Director

Betty moved into the community a decade ago to take this job; she is directed by her board to coordinate human service delivery in this rural region.

The Tri-County Community Improvement Project is a nonprofit United Way agency providing a wide spectrum of human services. The agency created a homeless shelter in an old warehouse with support from Good Foods, Inc., a major employer in the Green Valley area.

In Rockville:

The Rockville Emergency Programs
Peter Olsen, Executive Director

Twenty-five years ago, Peter founded the Rockville Emergency Programs for young people who were dropping out or in crisis. Since then, Peter has built an infrastructure of emergency services.

A joint agreement between the City of Rockville and Rockville State College governs Rockville Emergency Programs, which include a homeless shelter. Both the city and the college provide specific financial support. They also have a service contract with the county.

In Metford:

The County Government
Marjorie Bear, Assistant Director of County Social Services

Marjorie moved to Metford last year to take this job. She is passionate about the need to provide for homeless people and deal with all their needs.

The county contracts with Metford Shelter and Rockville Emergency Programs to provide shelters. But the economy is difficult. Three years ago Good Foods, Inc., shut down two canning lines, and everywhere people hear rumors of more shutdowns coming soon. The county board has slashed social services, and the budget continues to look bleak.

Metford Shelter
Wil Gaston, Executive Director

Wil has been director for three years and is currently creating a specialized facility for people who are homeless and have a mental illness.

Metford Shelter has an ongoing contract with the county, receives United Way funding, and has some operational support from the Good Foods Foundation. In this way the shelter has grown from ten beds to fifty beds in less than a decade.

Tri-County United Way
Kim Lee, President

Kim is the chair, having moved here three years ago as part of a management transfer within Good Foods, Inc.

The Tri-County United Way has always provided a modest level of support to local programs but has never been very aggressive either in fundraising or in dictating how local agencies use their allocations.

The Story

STAGE 1:
Envision Results by Working
Individual-to-Individual

Bring People Together
(Challenge 1A, p. 46)

Spring, Year One

After a mix-up resulted in turning away some families whom the Tri-County shelter could have served, Betty Jackson called Wil Gaston of Metford Shelter to talk about the problem. Because the possibilities excited them, they wanted to involve others. Wil suggested Betty call others.

Betty called Kim Lee, president of the United Way, and Marjorie Bear, Assistant Director of County Social Services. The ideas inspired both Kim and Marjorie, too, and each talked with Betty about others they could invite to a meeting.

As Betty and Kim worked on a final list, Kim mused, "We don't need a crowd, but we do need people who know about the challenges we face in the county. And we need people with the power to act."

After drafting their list of participants, Betty called Marjorie.

"Oh, no," Marjorie groaned, "Do we really want George? He always seems so negative; I'm afraid he'll turn people off at the first meeting."

While Betty agreed, she knew the group would need to involve George at some time. "Let's get him in on the ground floor and work on him," she proposed.

Betty, Kim, and Marjorie jointly sent out invitations, an agenda, and a membership roster to the people they had discussed. Fifteen people showed up.

For the first meeting Betty brought refreshments, which quickly became a ritual. Marjorie chaired the meeting. She and Betty had set the agenda: identify problems in serving homeless people. The participants wanted to explore collaboratively how to address these problems.

At the beginning of the first meeting, the group first set ground rules around starting times, regular participation, and confidentiality. Then they became involved in a discussion that dealt not with possibilities but with the existing programs. During the meeting, individual participants expressed surprise about the make up of the programs already in place. For instance, most of them hadn't known that Betty's Tri-County Community Improvement Project involved public health nurses.

"It's clear," said Marjorie, "that we don't truly know one another's programs. Perhaps the first order of business is to get that understanding." Peter suggested that program people come to the meetings to explain the services in some detail.

Betty complained, "There's so much to be done. We have to move more quickly!" Despite Betty's protests, the group designated three meetings to share program information.

The special meetings helped the members gather some basic information, but, by the third meeting, attendance was low. To counter this, Marjorie organized a conference call with Betty, Wil, and Kim. Together they mapped out the next meeting. First, the four of them would present the pertinent information that the participants had shared in the three special meetings. Then the participants would talk about what each organization and individual needed to get out of this joint effort.

Marjorie sent the agenda to all the group members and asked them to consider what they wanted from this collaborative effort. Betty, Wil, and Kim called the participants to encourage maximum attendance.

The next meeting proved so successful that the four conveners were positive that the effort was worth the extra time they were spending. The members expressed surprise at services they had not known about and identified some clear gaps in services.

Next, they each said how they expected to benefit from the collaboration— their self-interests. Wil openly admitted that the collaboration would be a feather in his hat. "This collaboration experience should help me get a better position when my family moves back East. And I want this idea to succeed, because I believe working together is the only way we're going to get things done in the future."

Enhance Trust
(Challenge 1B, p. 53)

Renew the Effort
(Challenge 3D, p. 110)

Enhance Trust
(Challenge 1B, p. 53)

Each group member discussed his or her reasons for working in collaboration, and, as the partners exposed their personal agendas, assumptions disappeared.

"If this is successful, it has to be good for your career, Marjorie, doesn't it?"

"Absolutely! You all know my boss will be retiring in the next three years, and I'm hoping to show the commissioners what kind of leader I can be."

With a greater sense of trust, everyone agreed to develop a mission statement the next time they met.

Resolve Conflicts
(Challenge 2B, p. 76)

The turnout for the next meeting was great! Eleven agencies each sent two people, and three client groups each sent representatives. However, conflict developed quickly. No sooner had Marjorie written the agenda on the flip chart than Peter snapped, "That agenda makes no sense! We need to focus on solving problems right now. The shelters are full to the max."

"You're out to stonewall us," asserted Wil.

"Wrong approach," countered Betty. "We don't know what Peter's thinking or why."

"In fact," said Kim, "let's try to find out what everyone's really thinking."

After much discussion, the group agreed to take more time to learn about everyone's needs. They talked further about organizational priorities, and the client representatives talked about the need for immediate help. While agreeing to balance present needs with future endeavors, the group determined two things they needed immediately if they were to move forward: (1) a vision statement to give everyone a shared sense of purpose, and (2) the mailing of meeting summaries to update the participants.

Confirm Our Vision
(Challenge 1C, p. 60)

Three weeks later, the group members quickly outlined a vision statement by brainstorming what they hoped the results of their collaboration would be. Two participants volunteered to forge these thoughts into vision and focus statements before the next meeting. They came back with the following:

> ### Our *Vision of Hope*
>
> *All homeless individuals or families in the Tri-County area will receive shelter, food, and emergency medical assistance at any emergency shelter in the area. On a daily basis, all organizations will coordinate available services with any client. A collaborative management structure will plan for future needs of the area.*

*Our **Focus***

Agencies working together to keep families together.

Excited by their accomplishments, the collaborative partners promptly began outlining specific results and strategies. They named their effort the "Tri-County Collaboration for Homeless Services." A small group agreed to refine the ideas and mail out the draft statements so everyone could review them before they met again. Everyone also agreed to bring letters of commitment from their individual boards or executives to the next meeting.

**Specify Desired Results
(Challenge 1D, p. 65)**

Shortly afterward, all the group members received the following draft in the mail. The letter listed the specific results and strategies that the small group had refined:

*The **result** of working together to address needs of homeless people will be:*

• *Shorter-term*

– *Provide up to seven days lodging for every homeless person and his or her family in the Tri-County area.*

– *Immediate access to the closest available bed for each homeless person.*

• *Longer-term*

– *Incidence of homelessness reduced by 30 percent in the next eight years.*

– *Public consciousness raised about what being a member of this community means, as shown by increased volunteer support at shelters and food shelves.*

*To achieve these results, our **strategies** are to:*

• *Make decisions, develop programs, and allocate resources collaboratively.*

• *Work with the county social service leadership to bring homeless issues to the top of the county board's agenda.*

• *Work with our personal contacts at the state legislature to develop support for funding and regulation of programs for this population.*

• *Create public education programs that address the core issues of homelessness, including exploitation of migrant workers, illiteracy, mental and physical health problems, and lack of awareness by the general public.*

STAGE 2:
Empower Ourselves by Working Individual-to-Organization

Summer, Year One

Everyone arrived at the next meeting full of ideas. After some discussion, one member expressed frustration.

"We've spent so much time talking about long-range possibilities," she complained, "that I haven't got anything to say to the clients in my shelter about what's going to happen for them right away!"

Her remark captured Peter's immediate interest. "I've got some funding ideas we haven't talked about. Let's work together on this new federal money that's available and get something done more quickly."

"No," Marjorie insisted. "We've done joint funding on small projects before. It's time for a truly new approach to the work we share in common. And that takes time and planning. We've got to stay centered on our collaborative mission."

Peter didn't respond; however, the other members agreed to take the time to do what they wanted to do in the way that would lead to success over the long-term. The needs were great, and everyone was tired of the band-aid approach. Someone made a joke about a tug of war and ending up in the mud, the tension eased, and Peter laughingly agreed that they needed to do long-range planning.

Confirm Organizational Roles (Challenge 2A, p. 72)

Then they talked about the letters of commitment they had obtained from various companies and boards: Betty and Wil had each secured authority to spend up to $2,000, and both had convened staff meetings to discuss the implications of the collaboration. The representative from Good Foods, Inc., had asked his boss to request a letter of support from the vice-president without stating any financial commitment.

One member of the collaborative team, a public health nurse, described the tedious step of going through channels to get her county's director to write a letter. Another member indicated that her board had offered to help secure funding. Peter related that his board was less sure of its commitment to such a new and radical approach.

Because two members were unable to obtain authorization, the group planned a strategy to influence those two organizations to make the needed commitments. They then agreed to copy the letters of commitment they had and distribute them among the respective organizations.

The discussion now moved to other concerns. Kim asked what role each organization and individual would play.

"Well," said Betty sheepishly, "I haven't got a computer or clerical time. I was happy to organize the first few meetings and bring refreshments, but I was hoping someone else would take on the job."

In response, one of the more candid members said what others were thinking: "Gee, Betty, if you can't even do this much, what can you do?"

"Not a lot," she responded. "Marjorie's got the whole county staff she can pull from, and Wil's got that new word processor. So it seems to me that one of them should be doing all this writing and mailing. What I bring to the table is a real connection to the migrant community, so maybe what I can do is marketing, you know, getting the word out once we get going. And I can help us make sure we keep clients involved."

"That's OK with me," said Wil. "If this is going to work, we need all the key players whether they're rich in resources or not. The real issue is what we all have to contribute. Let's take a few minutes to refresh our memories about what each of us brings."

At the next meeting, the group explored how to get the work done and agreed on the following:

- The twelve organizations that had been present for most of the meetings would be the primary collaborative members.

- The "leadership group" would stay intact as a steering committee, which would oversee and coordinate all the activities. This group included Marjorie, Wil, and Betty.

- Members would divide into three teams: resources, planning, and communications. Each group would write specific accountability and work plans and report back to the whole group.

For the remainder of the meeting, the members divided into these groups and agreed on individual roles. The steering committee spent the time writing up the collaborative structure.

At the next meeting, one member of the Resource Team shared his concerns: "I heard people talking about getting a lot of money from some magic grant, but that's not realistic. Frankly, I'm worried about agreeing to some big project anyway without trying something small first. With something under our belts, we'd know this collaboration is really going to work, and we'd have proof to give potential funders."

Resolve Conflicts
(Challenge 2B, p. 76)

Bring People Together
(Challenge 1A, p. 46)

Organize the Effort
(Challenge 2C, p. 82)

**Support the Members
(Challenge 2D, p. 88)**

Marjorie wasn't prepared for the sudden verbal explosion that greeted these comments. Clearly the group stood divided about what to do, and Marjorie was worried about how to keep things on track.

"Let's talk first about how to make this decision and then make the decision itself," Marjorie suggested. "In fact, let's talk about how to make all our decisions." She took the marker and moved to the flip chart.

The meeting went overtime, and tempers ran hot, then cold, then just plain tired. Two people said they wouldn't return: a community member who wanted action, not talk, and a student who said he felt "out of it." But finally, the partners agreed to the types of decisions they had to make, who would make these decisions, and how much authority each decision maker had.

Next, the group reviewed the work of the communication team. The members wanted to make sure that the team's plan clearly conveyed the decision-making process. The partners also talked about what each person needed in order to feel rewarded. Finally, the group outlined pilot projects they wanted to attempt. At the conclusion of this lengthy August meeting, the group members felt that finally, after nearly six months of work, they were on the brink of serving homeless people. Collaboration was a new technique for them, but they were getting the work done!

**STAGE 3:
Ensure Success by Working
Organization-to-Organization**

Fall, Year Two

A year passed quickly; output was high. The group implemented plans, piloted and evaluated projects, and measured results. Peter, who appreciated concrete actions, became fully involved in the action plan:

1. *Develop collaboration and collaborative decision making by organizing ourselves through regular meetings.*

2. *Agree upon and use the same computerized database system in our shelters.*

3. *Get each of the shelters in the Tri-County on line.*

4. *Procure vans and cars for transporting clients.*

5. *Develop food service programs with local providers.*

6. *Develop physical and mental health programs with local providers.*

7. *Continue to bring other organizations into our collaboration and keep it fresh and revitalized.*

The resource team coordinated volunteers, wrote and received a small grant, and collected information about foundations interested in collaborative approaches to providing shelter. Meanwhile, the planning team did the detailed work of identifying and pricing computer hardware and software that would enable shelters to be on-line. The members and the teams made decisions quickly.

During that fall, the steering committee made sure the right hand knew what the left was doing. The collaborative members had agreed to meet infrequently as a whole group, but after a few weeks they complained about isolation. So the steering committee hosted meetings every two months for the whole membership. These meetings provided a platform for the communications team to tell all the group members what everyone was doing.

Policies were a big part of the agenda at the first meeting of all the members. "Clients are telling me they get one story from the intake people at Rockville and another in Metford," said one person.

"And my understanding of our exchange program is different from an intake worker at your shelter, Peter," said another.

"I think we have policy issues we need to address," said Betty, "and a need for common intake procedures."

On the flip chart, Kim began listing all the daily snafus and the bigger system-wide problems the staff members were encountering. One member openly thanked Kim for demonstrating shared leadership by picking up the marker and moving the group forward.

The group then split that list into two action areas: implementation issues, which the collaborative partners could address through training or better communications; and policy issues, which each organization's board or governing body could address. The steering committee agreed to enlist representatives from various boards to draft joint policies. Each governing body would then have to ratify the policy agreements.

Like a dark rain cloud, evaluation of the work they had done loomed over everyone's head, and no one knew just how to approach this aspect of their collaborative work. The steering committee asked the members to come to the next meeting prepared to evaluate the pilot projects by considering three questions: (1) How financially viable was this effort? (2) What were the consumers' reactions? (3) Were they better served by having transportation to other shelters?

Manage the Work
(Challenge 3A, p. 96)

Organize the Effort
(Challenge 2C, p. 82)

Resolve Conflicts
(Challenge 2B, p. 76)

Create Joint Systems
(Challenge 3B, p. 102)

Evaluate the Results
(Challenge 3C, p. 106)

At the next meeting, they learned that their projects had yielded uneven results. The projects set up by the group had met the needs of some, but not all, clients. To justify the work and the expense, the group clearly needed to expand the effort or else drop it.

"We've got some new information now," said Wil, "and we need to redesign some of our plans."

Gradually, the collaborative partners designed and piloted other evaluation procedures. They used client surveys, funder questionnaires, and financial reviews to measure success. Many of the evaluations were very positive, but results really became clear when the partners pooled information:

- One member had postponed buying computers until the collaboration could decide what to do. The pressure from this agency helped speed up the decision process.

- Board members from another partner's organization attended a joint meeting, and policies about intake, funding, referral, and data privacy opened the door for streamlining regulations.

- Staff at the various organizations were enthusiastically sharing programming ideas, and many individuals reported feeling "like we're really starting to make a difference."

- A state senator took notice of the effort and supported new laws concerning funding for homeless shelters.

**Renew the Effort
(Challenge 3D, p. 110)**

Despite these positive results, many of the collaborative partners reported feeling overwhelmed. Kim put the issue clearly on the table: "We've proven that collaboration works," she said. "But actually doing program work is getting more difficult. It's as if the collaboration is becoming an unpaid part-time job for many of us. We need program workers now—and we need new blood. We also need to find out if all partners want to continue being involved."

Kim's comments sparked ongoing dialogue. As a result, each shelter identified one staff person to work full-time providing care and coordinating programs. In addition, two new organizations paid for part-time positions to staff the collaboration. Each organization committed to this arrangement for six months, freeing the funding team to seek moneys to support the collaborative work plan, buy computers, and pay for transportation.

Next, the collaborative team issued a report that documented the following changes:

1. *Shelter occupancy averaged 90 percent at each facility each week, up from 70 percent a year earlier.*
2. *Shelters were beginning to save money by eliminating a staff position through coordinated work.*
3. *The United Way had announced fiscal support.*
4. *Foundation awards had supplied computer equipment.*
5. *Automobile dealerships had donated minivans, so the volunteer driving program had ballooned.*
6. *The food shelves had gone on-line so that they could distribute surplus foodstuffs.*

Wanting to celebrate the success of their collaboration, the steering committee threw a holiday party for the partners, agency staff, and key community people. Marjorie nudged Wil when a performer satirized shelter administrators during the staff skit. The Rotary Club honored the collaboration with an award for community leadership, and a rousing hand of applause greeted the "first round" evaluation report. Achieving the mission had taken almost two years, but agencies in Green Valley, Rockville, and Metford were now implementing it successfully!

Winter's End, Year Two

The communications task team had done its work. Everyone was telling stories about how the collaboration could slay giants. The group had done the almost impossible: it had improved shelter services, and its long arm reached from the Tri-County area to the state capitol. Funders knew about the collaboration. The media were willing to cover this story. It was news! The joint effort had a marketing plan that worked.

While Marjorie was talking to Kim and Wil, she said, "Let's have a retreat to talk about the year-end evaluation results. It'll be a good time to reflect on all we've done and to create a succession plan to pass on leadership, since it's been almost two years since we started this. We need to get more of the field professionals involved, and the schools have a part to play."

The collaboration decided to have a day-long retreat, and the planning task force invited all the members and encouraged each one to bring a board member or senior staff.

STAGE 4:
Endow Continuity by Working Collaboration-to-Community

Create Visibility
(Challenge 4A, p. 119)

Involve the Community
(Challenge 4B, p. 123)

At the retreat, the partners reviewed the formal results of the evaluation. By the time they finished grappling with the succession plan, Peter had been elected chair. Then Marjorie called for ideas to generate new interest and attract new resources for homeless people.

"I've been thinking," said one new member. "One of the root problems of homelessness is the cycle of poverty inflicted on the children. Is there some way to get the schools in our Tri-County area more responsive to the needs of homeless elementary-aged kids?" The brainstorming that followed this request excited everyone.

After lunch, Kim began a discussion about increasing collaboration among the other human service providers in the Tri-County area. Using the work of the communications team as a base, the retreat participants broke into small groups to plan how to train other staff in existing shelters, educate the community to promote partnerships to serve shelter clients, and convince the legislature to reward agencies who saved money by working together.

Change the System
(Challenge 4C, p. 129)

As the afternoon continued, Peter said, "I believe we're really talking about going beyond help for homeless people to preventing homelessness altogether. Let me tell you about an idea for affordable housing I've been kicking around with my board chair. It won't be easy. We'd need to involve an awful lot of players, and we're talking about much more than two years to make this happen."

When Peter had described his plan, Kim was excited. "Let's get into small, issue-related groups," she advised. "We can start brainstorming today and plan how to get others involved in really making changes. Let's talk about the involvement of the legislators, educators, and the business community."

The board members also spoke up, voicing support for the kind of system-wide changes the collaborative partners wanted to work on. Within minutes, Betty was challenging these board members: "How can you leverage your power and position as board chairs and as important community leaders to help us get at the complexity of these problems? Is there some way you can meet and start co-planning programs that impact the whole person and the whole family?" The chairs agreed to think through this approach to making real changes on a broad level.

End the Collaboration
(Challenge 4D, p. 133)

As the group broke for dinner, Peter talked to Kim, Marjorie, Wil, and Betty. Peter was worried now that the group had elected him chair. "I'm concerned about taking over the reins from you, Marjorie," Peter said candidly. "You and Kim did a lot to keep this group in the eye of the power brokers in our counties."

"Now that the system has started to change," countered Marjorie, "it needs professionals like the three of you, well-versed in homeless issues. But there are things that Kim and I can do to help you adapt to the leadership role that's carved out for you." They were all so engrossed in planning that they almost missed getting anything to eat. Even as they filled their plates, they talked.

Dinner was only passable, but nothing could mar the event. The collaborative partners and board members made speeches. Some, serious, lauded the work of the collaboration. Some, in good humor, laughed and cried over two years of intense work. With so many new people involved, the collaboration had come full circle. In fact, the agenda for the next meeting of all the members called for reviewing ground rules and looking at the self-interest of everyone. But now the time had come to stand around the piano and sing in harmony—mostly!

◆ ◆ ◆

This story comes from real experiences of collaboration. Of course, many kinds of get-togethers and many, many phone calls happened in the time between the regular meetings. People met not only at the collaborative table but also with staff in their own organizations. Many other players became involved in specific tasks and withdrew when their work was finished.

What we discovered in the story are examples of creating, sustaining, and enjoying collaboration. Now let's look at more parts and greater detail. ◆

> 66
> *Time gives good advice.*
> — *Maltese proverb*
> 99

PART

II

How Do We Set Forth?

Let's Check the Lay of the Land

How Do We Set Forth?

Let's Check the Lay of the Land

Because collaboration can be complex, this book asks more of us than following a straight path. Therefore, we must know where we are and where we're going. To begin, we'll define collaboration. Then we will explore a metaphor that provides a useful framework for collaboration.

Understand Collaboration

In popular use, a collaboration occurs anytime people work together to achieve a goal. For our purposes, collaboration will be more narrowly defined. One element of that definition is the intensity of effort required by real collaboration. A brief story illustrates this:

Someone calls and says, "We can get a much stronger impact if we collaborate on this project."

"Great, let's meet," is the response.

After three meetings, our colleague is talking about the mission for the collaboration and what we all can achieve together in the next year .

Some of us were thinking, "Year? All we ever planned to give this was half-a-dozen meetings at the most." Trouble!

> **"**
> *If you do what you've always done, you'll get what you've always gotten.*
> — *Anonymous*
> **"**

Our colleague had a different concept of collaboration and the intensity of work it required. The following table shows a continuum of increasing intensity for building relationships and doing work:

	Cooperation*	Coordination	Collaboration
Key Relationships and Work	Shorter-term informal relations that exist without any clearly defined mission, structure, or planning effort characterize cooperation. Cooperative partners share information only about the subject at hand. Each organization retains authority and keeps resources separate so virtually no risk exists.	More formal relationships and understanding of missions distinguish coordination. People involved in a coordinative effort focus their longer-term interaction around a specific effort or program. Coordination requires some planning and division of roles and opens communication channels between organizations. While authority still rests with individual organizations, everyone's risk increases. Power can be an issue. Resources are made available to participants and rewards are shared.	A more durable and pervasive relationship marks collaboration. Participants bring separate organizations into a new structure with full commitment to a common mission. Such relationships require comprehensive planning and well-defined communication channels operating on all levels. The collaborative structure determines authority, and risk is much greater because each partner contributes its resources and reputation. Power is an issue and can be unequal. Partners pool or jointly secure the resources, and share the results and rewards.
Examples	One group of Southeast Asian Mutual Assistance Associations meets each month to exchange information on service approaches. They update each other on the latest techniques, on pending changes in legislation, and on which funders are likely to support their program types.	The Council of Agency Executives meets monthly to help the United Way plan for human service delivery. This often requires more than the exchange of information because the participants must work out philosophical differences and agree on a range of plans. But they do not share the vision of a larger purpose.	A group of Hispanic organizations comes together to address the need for job development and job training. They are looking at long-term plans to develop businesses that will provide jobs. They will involve government training services (to help secure grants and provide job training) and post-secondary institutions (for academic and vocational education).
Intensity (risk, time needed, opportunity)	lower intensity ➡️		higher intensity

* *Different authors use cooperation and coordination interchangeably. This book follows the work of Sharon Kagan, in defining the least intense level as cooperation. Used with permission from Sharon L. Kagan,* United We Stand: Collaboration for Child Care and Early Education Services. *(New York: Teachers College Press, copyright 1991 by Teachers College, Columbia University. All rights reserved.), pp. 1–3.*

Regardless of the intensity, many groups call themselves collaborations. They also use such terms as alliance, coalition, partnership, and so on. As a result, confusion exists about what the word collaboration means. Moreover, some groups enter into collaboration when they need only cooperate with each other or coordinate activities. Other groups do need collaboration but do not understand the intensity of effort it will demand.

As defined in this book, collaboration is the most intense way of working together while still retaining the separate identities of the organizations involved. The beauty of collaboration is the acknowledgment that each organization has a separate and special function, a power that it brings to the joint effort. At the same time, each separate organization provides valuable services or products often critical to the health and well-being of their community.

Joint Efforts—A Word by Any Other Name

Joint efforts go by many names. If all members agree on a higher level of intensity of work, many of these efforts can be collaborations whatever they're called. At the same time, the group, however it is named, can be very successful, even though working less intensely. Two elements are crucial to successful joint efforts: everyone must agree on the level of intensity and the level of intensity must be appropriate to the desired results. Here are some names for joint efforts.

- **Advisory Committee:** provides suggestions and assistance at the request of an organization.

- **Alliance:** a union or connection of interests that have similar character, structure, or outlook; functions as a semiofficial organization of organizations.

- **Coalition:** a temporary alliance of factions, parties, and so on for some specific purpose; mobilizes individuals and groups to influence outcomes.

- **Commission:** a body authorized to perform certain duties or steps or to take on certain powers; generally appointed by an official body.

- **Competition:** the act of seeking to gain that for which another is also striving; rivalry; a contest; nonetheless a form of joint effort.

- **Confederation:** being united in an alliance or league; joining for a special purpose.

- **Consolidation:** combining of several into one; usually implies major structural changes that bring operations together.

- **Consortium:** association; same as alliance.

- **Cooperation:** the act of working together to produce an effect.

- **Coordination:** working to the same end with harmonious adjustment or functioning.

- **Federation:** the act of uniting by agreement of each member to subordinate its power to that of the central authority in common affairs.

- **Joint Powers:** the act by legally constituted organizations (such as governmental agencies or corporations) of assigning particular powers each has to a mutually defined purpose; a written document, called a joint powers agreement, spells out the relationship between the groups.

- **League:** a compact for promoting common interests; an alliance.

- **Merger:** the legal combining of two or more organizations; the absorption of one interest by another.

- **Network:** individuals or organizations formed in a loose-knit group.

- **Partnership:** an association of two or more who contribute money or property to carry on a joint business and who share profits or losses; a term loosely used for individuals and groups working together.

- **Task Force:** a self-contained unit for a specific purpose, often at the request of an overseeing body, that is not ongoing.

"

You must be the change you wish to see.

— *Mahatma Gandhi (1869–1948) Leader of the Indian nationalist movement*

"

Given the greater intensity, the investment in collaboration must be worth the effort. This is because collaboration changes the way we work. We must move from:

- Competing ——→ to building consensus.

- Working alone ——→ to including others from a diversity of cultures, fields, and sectors.

- Thinking mostly about activities, services, and programs ——→ to thinking also about larger results and strategies.

- Focusing on short-term accomplishments ——→ to demanding long-term results.

Above all, collaboration has to pay attention to language. We concentrate on what "we" want over and above what individual partners want. Listening to each other and thinking creatively become all-important.

Given the variety of joint efforts and the intensity of collaboration, these authors define collaboration as follows:

> **Collaboration is a mutually beneficial and well-defined relationship entered into by two or more organizations to achieve results they are more likely to achieve together than alone.**

In this definition, organizations may be formal or informal groups or constituencies, legally incorporated or not. Of course, individuals working alone can also be part of a collaboration, and input from individuals in the community is essential. Yet, if individuals want to make an impact, they usually must represent an organization or community of some kind.

The story of the Tri-County collaboration revealed benefits for the individual partners and also for the organizations that the group members represented. Wil felt that his work on the joint effort might result in a better job when he moved back East; Marjorie hoped for a promotion. The organizations ended up meeting the needs of their clients in a much more focused way than in the past. Everyone involved in the collaboration knew that the members and organizations could not, and would not, have achieved these results alone.

Since the definition this book offers for collaboration implies greater intensity, we need to understand when to be cautious—when that greater intensity might make things worse, not better. The factors that make or break collaboration include *ideology, leadership, power, history, competition, and resources.*

Ideology: Sometimes organizations have substantial ideological differences and misunderstandings. Debates on values and beliefs often leave little room for the flexibility crucial to collaboration.

Leadership: If no one has enough power to bring the needed organizations together, people will quickly disband. If the wrong person leads meetings, the group might fail. A brief story illustrates the point:

> *Foundations, businesses, and child-care organizations met to provide more comprehensive and affordable child care. The recently retired executive of a large agency chaired the group. He divided the group into two sections: one for the more established institutions that controlled funds and the other for the child-care providers. This second group tended to be women and people of color who did not have money.*
>
> *The executive reasoned that each group could plan for its needs and contributions in relation to a common mission. But the result was bitter feuding between the two groups, each of which came to have a separate identity. Leadership makes a difference!*

Power: Power is rarely equal among members of a collaboration. Yet we can equally value different powers. Successful collaborations find ways to balance the inequities among all members. If, however, one person can take unilateral action or if a substantial difference in power exists, the group cannot achieve an essential melding of power.

History: The issues the group faces may be threatening because of historical disagreement. Or past efforts may have been ineffective. If this history exists, then collaboration is more difficult to accomplish without a great deal of preparation.

Competition: Too often organizations come together simply to obtain resources for existing efforts—for instance, funders *require* a collaboration. Or organizations believe that if they work together they will more likely get funds. Thus, the underlying reason for the joint effort is money. Basically, the organizations still go it alone to compete for funds. If dollars do not flow readily, the inherent competition can destroy the joint effort.

Resources: The potential member organizations may be unable to contribute what is needed for the collaboration. For example, one or more groups cannot send representatives; the time required causes such internal hardship that an organization sees costs outweighing benefits; or an organization cannot handle the requirements because of lack of skills or because the joint effort creates too much information to manage.

> 66
>
> *Nothing in life is to be feared. It is only to be understood.*
>
> — *Madame Curie (1867–1934) Polish-French physicist*
>
> 99

> 66
>
> *Do not call for black power or green power. Call for brain power.*
>
> — *Barbara Jordan Texas Congresswoman*
>
> 99

"

*No one can
go it alone.*

— *Grace Gil Olibvarez*
Mexican American social
activist/attorney

"

Finally, we must ask ourselves, Given these factors, should we collaborate at all? What is our likelihood of success? We don't want to try the impossible. On the other hand, we don't want these problems to scare us off. Maybe collaboration under these circumstances will work with a special effort.

Members in a collaboration never agree unanimously on all matters. In fact, disagreement is both healthy and desirable. But successful collaborations find ways to work together; members experience rewards as they build dynamic relationships needed to do the desired work.

How are collaborations formed? Through someone's initiation, through someone's directive, or through legal mandate. However they begin, collaborations require patience, creativity, and sophisticated skills with people. Patience is especially called for if we are to commit to collaboration. To build that commitment, we need two crucial items: a change in our thinking and a common language, one that gives us new symbols of what is important.

Explore a Metaphor

Let's view collaboration through the metaphor of a journey, that is, a *destination* toward which *travelers* move together on a *road* they build.

We can find this metaphor in our definition of collaboration: "a mutually beneficial and well-defined relationship entered into by two or more organizations to achieve results they are more likely to achieve together than alone." This definition outlines (1) the *destination*—achieving results (2) that the *travelers*—the collaborating organizations—move toward (3) on the *road*—building well-defined relationships and accomplishing mutually beneficial work.

Seek a Destination

The destination of our journey is results. For the collaboration as a whole, the destination is the achievement of *community benefits*. (For our purposes, a community is any group united by geography, population, practice, religion, business, or other form of shared culture.) For a particular organization or an individual, the destination is fulfillment of individual *self-interests*.

Seek a Destination

Community Benefits

When Betty and Wil talked about the issues involved in helping homeless people in the Tri-County story, they set out on a collaborative journey that brought community benefits for farm laborers, migrants, young people, and families who were homeless. In addition, within their own organizations, Betty and Wil became better able to access government programs and to provide drug treatment, health care, and mental health services. Thus, the community benefits of their collaboration were many and varied. Here are five other examples of collaborations working for their communities:

- *An agency serving urban youth recognized that many young people do not receive post-secondary academic or vocational education. To create a community-wide effort to provide youth with a pathway to further education, the agency formed a collaboration of twenty-six people representing business, community education, higher education, vocational training, public schools, teachers' unions, and city government.*

- *On the East Coast, more than twenty groups—churches, businesses, health care and human service organizations—came together to reduce an infant mortality rate that was considerably higher than the national average.*

> **"**
> *Two heads,*
> *four eyes.*
> — *A saying of the Igbo people of Nigeria*
> **"**

"

*We must do the things
we think we cannot do.
The future belongs
to those who believe
in the beauty
of their dreams.*

— *Eleanor Roosevelt
(1884–1962)
Humanitarian,
U. N. Delegate*

"

- *Members of a neighborhood business association watched their neighborhood and businesses decline. The typical promotions didn't work. To revitalize the neighborhood, they are bringing businesses, government agencies, arts organizations, and non-profit social service agencies together to create measurable results, both short- and long-term.*

- *People from agencies serving Native Americans know firsthand that for many reasons their clients have great difficulty obtaining mental health services. They want to develop a community-supported network that cultivates the mental, emotional, and spiritual health of American Indians.*

- *Organizers in an African American community see that many people in their neighborhoods are chronically discouraged. The organizers believe that providing more services won't work. They believe the solution is to articulate, communicate, and reinforce African American community values and assist individuals and institutions in the African American community to further economic development and community building.*

Communities work to achieve a variety of dreams—their destinations:

- Human service nonprofits improve the lives of individuals and families.

- Arts organizations stimulate creativity.

- Schools educate by providing people with information and skills.

- Health care agencies heal and prevent illness.

- Environmental organizations protect and improve the surroundings.

- Businesses produce products or services to sell, provide jobs, and pay taxes.

- Government protects the health and safety of its citizens.

Collaborations can increase the potential benefits of these efforts.

Each collaboration has its own unique destination of community benefits. Yet each member within the collaboration also brings along her or his separate self-interests.

Self-Interests

Human beings combine opposites within themselves: All are altruistic; all are self-interested. Producing benefits for the community motivates us. But meeting our own self-interests is equally motivating.

For instance, a business person becomes a partner in the collaboration because participation demonstrates support for the community, buys good will, and increases business. Or a government official, accused of being power hungry, collaborates to demonstrate inclusiveness.

Let's examine self-interests by returning to our Tri-County story. After meeting a few times, Wil openly acknowledged that the collaboration would help him get a better job back East. Marjorie, too, had a personal desire. Her boss was retiring within three years, and she was eager to display her leadership.

Can self-interest work for a collaboration? Yes, but better when the partners admit to it. Members must ask, directly, "What will we each get out of this?"

A brief scenario illustrates the point:

> *After five meetings, the work and details bogged down the group members. The consultant they hired asked each to say what she or he wanted from the collaboration.*
>
> - *One person from a major institution stated that he wanted to develop the program the collaboration had been discussing and was looking to write a major grant for it.*
>
> - *Another person revealed that if the program was funded, she wanted to staff it.*
>
> - *All the other participants admitted that they endorsed the effort, were willing to write support letters, but would not gain anything directly.*
>
> *The result? The group wrote the letters and never met again. Self-interests and community benefits did not mesh.*

On the other hand, the Tri-County story detailed how Peter wanted to solve problems immediately. Rather than resulting in dissolution of the collaboration, his impatience led to a discussion of organizational priorities, a vision statement, and a commitment to desired and shared results. The members resolved their conflicts and journeyed to a destination of mutually achieved results. Here, self-interest and community benefits meshed and worked out beautifully.

> 66
>
> *Self-interest is the prime mover of people.*
>
> — *Saul Alinsky (1909–1972) Community activist*
>
> 99

> 66
>
> *There are three kinds of groups: Those which make things happen; those which wait for things to happen; and those which wonder what happened.*
>
> — *Anonymous*
>
> 99

Self-interest is always present, so we must recognize and acknowledge it. If we don't, we lose our way on the collaborative journey. We'll revisit self-interest in Part III.

◆ ◆ ◆

Community benefits and individual self-interests draw us forward; they are our destination, the end of the long road. These community benefits and self-interests guide our relationships and focus our work. Next, let's look at ourselves as travelers who journey together toward our destination.

Become Travelers

The image of the rugged individual may have worked when new frontiers continually opened to provide escape for adventuresome pioneers. But the frontiers have disappeared, and we look at collaboration as a new way of relating and working. For some people, however, collaboration has been an essential part of their history and their lives. For them, working together is not new.

Whether collaboration is new or familiar, we must see ourselves as global partners who harness our diversity to travel together toward a shared destination. To learn from our diversity we must acknowledge each person and benefit from her or his *customs, languages, preferences,* and *powers.*

Become Travelers

Customs

We each have customs that we understand but seem foreign to others. In the United States, midwesterners tend to call colleagues by their first name as a sign of friendliness. Yet in many African American communities, respect is shown by using last names and titles. People on the eastern seaboard arch their eyebrows at the suggestion of a seven thirty breakfast meeting—nine is the preferred starting time. In the Midwest, however, early meetings are common. Native Americans often begin their meetings by sharing food before business gets started—they are building relationships. To others, eating before working seems unproductive. "Get on with the business at hand," they say.

To journey with fellow travelers, we must prepare ourselves for customs and values that differ from ours. Acceptance and acknowledgment of different customs build the trust essential to effective collaboration.

Languages

English, Spanish, Swahili, or Hmong are recognizable as different languages. "Personal" languages are not so easy to distinguish. For example:

- *The word "collaboration" means different kinds of relationships. One person may envision a long-term commitment; another only a few meetings.*

- *Many businesses use the term "Total Quality Management" to mean seeing everyone, internal and external to the company, as customers. But how does a nonprofit define production and customers? In fact, some nonprofits ridicule the use of the word "customer" as inappropriate to their work.*

- *The legislature passes a bill that speaks of empowerment. The government agency responsible for implementing the bill comes up with regulations on compliance. Double-speak? Maybe not. Still, how can any real change take place when everyone hears something different?*

To journey with fellow travelers, we must learn each other's language, examine the popular buzz words, and define our terms.

> **"**
> *. . . one only understands that with which one agrees.*
> — *Kaygusuz Abdal*
> *15th century Arab Ashik*
> **"**

> **"**
> *If you have your language and you have your culture, and you're not ashamed of them, then you know who you are.*
> — *Maria Urquides*
> *American educator*
> **"**

> *Let the world know you as you are, not as you think you should be, because sooner or later, if you are posing, you will forget the pose, and then where are you?*
>
> — Fanny Brice
> (1891–1951)
> American comedienne
> and singer

Preferences

Taking the time to learn different languages might not fit our preferred way of relating and working. For example, some prefer to explore the mystery of another's language; others are drawn by the magnetism of immediate action.

But let's admit at the outset that our preference depends on the situation, and we tend to cycle through different preferences, emphasizing one or two. We can look at four personal preferences: *begetting, becoming, being, and bequeathing:*

- **Begetting:** Some people enjoy a time of rapid growth and very high energy. They enjoy exploring, discovering, and uncovering creativity and potential in themselves and others. Because begetting people usually do not like to deal with detail, they may consider policies and procedures unimportant. *Begetting people continually seek out options to make their dreams come true.*

- **Becoming:** Other people prefer to focus. They recognize that the group must shed some goals and hone others. They like the time of blending ideas and making choices, but policies and procedures interest them at only a minimal level. *Becoming people concern themselves with focusing the collective vision to make something happen.*

- **Being:** Some people enjoy taking pride in their achievements. They focus on productivity. Because policies and procedures are important to them, these people want to write everything down. They like to function smoothly with organization; for them, administration is key. *Being people have a sense that their group "has arrived."*

- **Bequeathing:** Still other people prefer the finish. They like to know that they have served or produced all they could. Secure and satisfied, they love to tell stories about the history of the collaboration. *Bequeathing people delight in imparting their wisdom and giving their resources to others to carry on or to begin something new.*

Mandated Collaborations?

Can we force people to be partners? We may want to yell a resounding "No!" but the truth is that federal, state, and local governments and funders are increasingly requiring collaborations. This can cause difficulties when someone from outside the collaboration determines the desired results, dictates who will lead, and decides who will be members.

Collaborations can work successfully under a mandate when (1) sufficient resources back up requirements; (2) pre-established goals are broad; (3) local capacity and will is supported; and (4) members of the collaboration can capitalize on and not be constrained by the mandate. Members of a collaboration can capitalize on a mandate when flexibility in goals, membership, and structure exist.

Adapted from the work of Sharon Kagan. Used with permission.

Here's a quick story to illustrate how these preferences work:

> *We're sitting at the table together. I repeatedly say, "We've got to brain-storm possible results for our collaboration!"*
>
> *My partner says, "No, we need to get clear on how we're going to proceed. Then we have to decide who's going to take the minutes!"*
>
> *While we might argue right and wrong about each other's recommendations, the conflict really involves our individual preferences: I prefer begetting; my partner prefers being.*

A healthy collaboration acknowledges that the group needs a diversity of preferences and that all these preferences are valuable. Only then can the collaboration plan a *sequence* of actions to best use the preferences each members claims. For example, we acknowledge time for brainstorming (begetting) to be followed by prioritizing and drafting a vision statement (becoming). Later, we acknowledge that we need to emphasize action planning (being) to be followed by building greater support in the community (bequeathing). These are matters of sequence, not right or wrong.

Powers

Besides claiming our preferences, we must declare our power. For many, *power* is a negative word meaning control, physical force, undue influence. Not an appealing scenario! Others think that power is connected to gender, race, age, culture. Strong patterns to break!

Yet power also means "the ability to do . . . having great influence." We all have some form of power; we just need to recognize it and use it intentionally. Collaborations unite and extend our various powers. As we collaborate, we decide where we want to go (destination); what each partner (traveler) wants; and how we are going to get what we want (the road). During the course of the collaboration, we devote our time to obtaining and spending power in the best interest of the community and ourselves.

How much power we have to spend depends, in part, on the availability of that power. People with a special skill have more power if they alone possess the skill. Yet, individuals and organizations have power only if we, the collaborative partners, value the specific power and are unable to obtain it from others. The problem is that some people accumulate power by not sharing their expertise and resources.

Power is always present and is never equal. However, in a collaboration we do not seek *equality*. Instead, we search for *equity*; we acknowledge and value the different types of power each person and organization bring to our joint effort.

> **"**
> *A person working alone has all the power of social dust.*
> — *Saul Alinsky (1909–1972) Community activist*
> **"**

Obviously, power penetrates all relationships and work. If we want our collaboration to be successful, we must openly claim the power we bring; be aware of our own corruptibility; refuse to deny our power; and resolve any conflicts that grow from the use of power.

If we do not embrace these four actions, we can fall into the shadow side of power. That is, we confuse the power to make something happen with the power to control others; we confuse obtaining and spending power with manipulation—the undeclared use of power.

As collaborative partners, we acknowledge and retain control over our own power. We refuse to consider one type of power as better than another. We form collaborations to unite and extend our various powers, eliminating none. This melding of power is our ideal. And we stretch our comfort level by exercising our own powers intentionally.

Sunshine and Shadow Powers

We can view power as both positive—moving things forward—and negative—holding things back:

Type	Sunshine Power	Shadow Power
Charisma	Charming others with enthusiasm and confidence	Seducing others
Connections	Making connections to others who are seen to have power	Controlling access to others who are seen to have power
Expertise	Applying knowledge, skills, information, and experience (including the experience of collaboration)	Withholding knowledge, skills, information, and experience, or being arrogant in applying these skills
Fame and visibility	Having a reputation acknowledged by others	Using a negative reputation to maintain or seize power by making people afraid
Integrity and credibility	Demonstrating consistency of action and words	Acting or speaking inconsistently so others don't know what to expect
Life experience	Describing life events as they apply to the situation so others can learn from the experiences, observations, and values	Withholding such information and/or complaining of being undervalued as an excuse for not contributing
Persuasion	Being able to convince others what to do	Bullying others into taking action or not
Position and "turf	Having clear boundaries as granted by a governing body or hierarchy, knowing how to go through channels, having security in a home-base	Remaining isolated, demanding that everything go through channels, requiring all activities to happen on one's home-base
Resources	Being able to reward, and choosing to do so	Withholding needed resources, or forcing others to jump through hoops to get them

◆ ◆ ◆

To harness our differences in customs, language, preferences, and powers, we refuse to debate who's right or who's wrong. Instead, we look at our destination and ask: How do our customs, languages, preferences, and powers help get us where we want to go?

Take to the Road

To reach our destination, we need a good road. Not one of gravel, concrete, or Tarmac, but of relationships to build and work to do. The road offers a number of challenges. Not obstacles, but opportunities; not potholes, but possibilities! As we travel this road, we'll note four distinct terrains that correspond to the **four stages** of collaboration. Within each stage, we'll face four **challenges** that build on each other over the course of our journey. Finally, we'll see that the road has a unique **shape**.

Take to the Road

Four Stages

Stage 1: Envision Results by Working Individual-to-Individual
Terrain: Hill Country

Collaborations begin individual-to-individual to envision results. Remember how Betty Jackson called Wil Gaston to talk about the issues of homelessness? The collaboration started with a conversation between two concerned people.

> **66**
>
> *We build the road and the road builds us.*
>
> *— Sri Lankan saying*
>
> **99**

Our collaboration may grow from a good idea we shared over the telephone or from a mandate issued by a funder or legislature. Whichever way, we get to know each other, attend meetings, and start to work. Together, *individual-to-individual,* we *envision* the desired results and keep the collaboration focused on our destination. But the ups and downs of starting a collaboration, of finding our roles as partners, are as strenuous as going through hill country.

Stage 2: Empower Ourselves by Working Individual-to-Organization
Terrain: Marshland

Collaborations continue along the road in an individual-to-organization relationship to empower their members. After going through hill country, the characters in the Tri-County story entered a marshland, where they started to get stuck. They realized they didn't have authority from their own organizations to act as easily as they wanted to. Some partners were able to obtain authorization from their organizations; others weren't. During the summer, they got into conflict with each other; they struggled to organize themselves.

When we enter this marshland, we are like the partners in the story: we need clear authority from our home-base organizations to work effectively together. We must also be clear about how we will work together. Clarity from *individual-to-organization* and within the collaboration *empowers* us to begin action. As Kim, Marjorie, Betty, Peter, and Wil discovered, we can avoid getting bogged down in the marshland.

Stage 3: Ensure Success by Working Organization-to-Organization
Terrain: Fertile Plains

Moving on in our collaboration, we relate organization-to-organization to ensure results. Now, to build relationships and work together, we find formal ways for our agencies to interact. After fifteen months, the Tri-County players built joint systems and policies that were the same from organization-to-organization; each shelter identified one staff person to work full-time providing care and coordinating programs; and two organizations paid for part-time positions to support the collaboration.

As we journey, we work *organization-to-organization to ensure success.* Like the key players in the Tri-County story, we begin to reap the benefit of what we have sown on these now fertile plains.

Stage 4: Endow Continuity by Working Collaboration-to-Community
Terrain: Broad Forest

Finally, as we complete our journey, we relate collaboration-to-community to endow continuity. The Tri-County travelers began to find ways to institutionalize their success in the community. With help from more people and organizations, they developed increased support so that their efforts would bring about new and continuing efforts along the road they had traveled.

After more than two years of traveling together—up the hill country, through the marsh land, across the fertile plains—the partners had now come to the shade, comfort, and resources of the broad forest. Marjorie passed leadership to Peter; more people became involved; the collaboration identified new resources and approached the legislature.

From *collaboration-to-community,* we garner increased support to *endow* the effort over time and to influence greater change in the systems that affect us all. The many seeds we have planted begin to grow into a broad forest. The building materials we need for continuity come from this broad forest.

Within each of these four terrains, or stages, we find four challenges that help build relationships and do the work of collaboration. Let's look at these.

> **"**
> *Relationship is a pervading and changing mystery.*
> — *Eudora Welty*
> *American author*
> **"**

Challenges

Within each of the four stages of collaboration, travelers face four challenges. Each challenge builds on the previous ones. Some collaborations may enjoy great success without meeting all of them. Yet creating, sustaining, and enjoying a collaboration is best accomplished by facing all the challenges.

Here are the challenges for each stage:

Stage 1: Envision Results by Working Individual-to-Individual
Challenges: Bring People Together (Challenge 1A)
Enhance Trust (Challenge 1B)
Confirm Our Vision (Challenge 1C)
Specify Desired Results (Challenge 1D)

Stage 2: Empower Ourselves by Working Individual-to-Organization
Challenges: Confirm Organizational Roles (Challenge 2A)
Resolve Conflicts (Challenge 2B)
Organize the Effort (Challenge 2C)
Support the Members (Challenge 2D)

Stage 3: Ensure Success by Working Organization-to-Organization
Challenges: Manage the Work (Challenge 3A)
Create Joint Systems (Challenge 3B)
Evaluate the Results (Challenge 3C)
Renew the Effort (Challenge 3D)

Stage 4: Endow Continuity by Working Collaboration-to-Community
Challenges: Create Visibility (Challenge 4A)
Involve the Community (Challenge 4B)
Change the System (Challenge 4C)
End the Collaboration (Challenge 4D)

The Shape

*Shape of
the road*

Whatever the challenges we face, we need to realize that this road is not really straight. The road twists and turns like a cloverleaf; it goes on, always returning to an intersection. What does this imply? While the focus of each stage is its four challenges, we meet all the challenges repeatedly and not necessarily in order. In the Tri-County story, the partners called three special meetings because they were bogged down while envisioning results (Stage 1). Yet many collaborations meet this challenge to renew the effort while ensuring success (Stage 3). Similarly, most groups face conflict while empowering their members (Stage 2) after some trust has been built, but Peter and Wil were already in conflict in Stage 1.

Don't be alarmed! We meet some challenges only briefly. And as we move around, we increase our skills. So the next time we face the same challenge, we're better prepared.

Pages 40–41 show what the road looks like with its four terrains and corresponding stages, challenges, and shape.

The collaborative journey is one of destination, travelers, and road.

What is our destination? That is, what are we hoping and working for? Community benefits and individual self-interests.

Who are we, the travelers? We are individuals and organizations who can harness the diversity of customs, language, preferences, and powers to achieve our destination.

On what road are we journeying? A road of developing relationships and successful work, with four stages, or terrains, and four challenges in each stage. Thus, we achieve our joint destination.

What does that road look like? The collaborative road is a cloverleaf. So we keep coming back to the an intersection, each time building on and improving what we're doing.

Let's return to our Tri-County story. When the partners met to celebrate their accomplishments (they had reached their destination), Betty challenged the board members to find an approach that would make real changes on a broad level. New possibilities and plans excited the collaboration. Their collaboration had come to both an ending and a beginning. The partners were ready to refine what they had done and to build on their success.

In our collaborative journey, the goals we discuss early on may be detailed later; members may change; structures that we laboriously work out in the beginning may later be modified or replaced by ones that better serve our ever-clearer purpose. As we travel the cloverleaf road, we discover that flexibility and adaptability are key to effective collaboration.

This cloverleaf road raises problems for service providers and funders who are accustomed to linear plans and well-defined goals. They want a straight road that goes from North to South, from beginning to end. Many service providers and funders want plans their members can complete in short time frames of one or two years. Collaborations, however, serve one purpose and one purpose only: to produce results that are more likely to be achieved by working together than by working alone. Collaborations do not exist to fulfill preexisting criteria for a clear beginning and a definite end.

If we travel alone, we choose our own route and our own timetable. If we travel with others, we need to blend and hone and modify our routes and our timetables. When our whole group goes together, we may not end up exactly where each person wanted to go. And even if we end up where each of us wanted to be, how we got there will not be precisely as planned and will usually take longer than imagined. But think of the community benefits and the self-satisfaction! We may not see the sight we set out for. Instead, we may discover the eighth wonder of the world—and we do this together. ◆

> 66
>
> *Aerodynamically, the bumble bee shouldn't be able to fly, but the bumble bee doesn't know it so it goes on flying anyway.*
>
> — *Mary Kay Ash cosmetics executive*
>
> 99

> 66
>
> *Happily may I walk. May it be beautiful before me. May it be beautiful behind me. May it be beautiful below me. May it be beautiful above me. May it be beautiful all around me. In beauty it is finished.*
>
> — *Navaho Night Chant*
>
> 99

Stage 1: Envision Results by Working Individual-to-Individual

Terrain:
Hill Country

Challenges:
Bring People Together (Challenge 1A)
Enhance Trust (Challenge 1B)
Confirm Our Vision (Challenge 1C)
Specify Desired Results (Challenge 1D)

Stage 4: Endow Continuity by Working Collaboration-to-Community

Terrain:
Broad Forest

Challenges:
Create Visibility (Challenge 4A)
Involve the Community (Challenge 4B)
Change the System (Challenge 4C)
End the Collaboration (Challenge 4D)

Stage 2: Empower Ourselves by Working Individual-to-Organization

Terrain:

Marshland

Challenges:

Confirm Organizational Roles (Challenge 2A)
Resolve Conflicts (Challenge 2B)
Organize the Effort (Challenge 2C)
Support the Members (Challenge 2D)

Stage 3: Ensure Results by Working Organization-to-Organization

Terrain:

Fertile Plains

Challenges:

Manage the Work (Challenge 3A)
Create Joint Systems (Challenge 3B)
Evaluate the Results (Challenge 3C)
Renew the Effort (Challenge 3D)

PART III

How Do We Journey Together?

Let's Explore the Four Stages of Collaboration

Stage 1: Envision Results by Working Individual-to-Individual

Managing the Ups and Downs of Hill Country

As the Tri-County story in Part I illustrates, the collaborative road begins by assembling people, building trust, creating a vision, and agreeing on desired results. Thus, Stage 1 resembles hill country because we must manage the ups and downs of starting together.

We begin the collaboration by bringing people together and building trust, individual-to-individual. The travelers may come from far and wide. Early on, we learn to trust these many and varied travelers; we rely on their integrity, their honesty, and their fairness. That's why disclosure of self-interests in relation to the destination is so important.

Besides trust, we need rituals—repeated actions. Rituals help us build a common language. They help us feel more comfortable with each other and provide a common ground so that together we can envision our destination and manage the journey.

For many of us, the word ritual connotes religious ceremonies and shadowy rites far removed from daily life. In reality, our lives are crammed with rituals. For instance, each of us has rituals around personal habits: when we shower; where we squeeze the toothpaste; what side of the bed we sleep on; what we drink while we read the daily newspaper. Our list of daily rituals is actually quite long.

Since ritual plays a significant role in our daily lives, collaborations must acknowledge and integrate them. Because a collaboration cannot include everyone's personal rituals, we must create common ones that build shared ownership. In the Tri-County story, everyone enjoyed sharing the refreshments Betty brought to each meeting. Around that ritual of eating, the group members did some of their best thinking!

Of course, we need trust and ritual throughout our collaborative journey; however, we focus on them as we envision results by working individual-to-individual. In this beginning of the journey, we face four challenges and learn how to:

Bring People Together

Enhance Trust

Confirm Our Vision

Specify Desired Results

Bring People Together (Challenge 1A)

Collaborations start when the members get to know each other and build trust by creating shared rituals. Sometimes we encounter racism, sexism, and classism and experience unequal power. Sometimes we learn to trust people we've avoided in the past.

Bring People Together

Knowing these difficulties, collaborations first bring the "right" people together. As one partner said, "This is a make or break item." The challenge of bringing people together requires the emerging collaboration to perform four steps:

1) **Have an Initiator**

2) **Choose Potential Members**

3) **Invite Participation**

4) **Take Time**

Have an Initiator

All collaborations begin with one or more initiators. They have a vision in mind; they reach out to others, explain the rationale, and recruit group members. In our Tri-County story, Betty Jackson, the executive director of the Community Improvement Project, called Wil Gaston of Metford Shelter to talk about the issues of the homeless. The possibilities excited them, and they decided to involve others.

Much depends on the initiators' ability to build trust. To do this, they must know themselves—understand their own customs, languages, preferences, and powers. (See pages 30–34 for information on customs, languages, preferences, and powers.)

The Tri-County story illustrates the difficulty: Betty wanted to involve George at the beginning rather than wait until the group was halfway down the road when she would have to explain (and possibly defend) the collaborative actions. She knew her preference here. But she protested when the group proposed three special meetings to explore the Tri-County services in detail. Here, Betty's language was of inclusion where others wanted limits. And she preferred creating the collaboration (begetting) over discussing details (being). (See page 32.)

Besides these understandings, the initiators must present the vision and the results that define it clearly enough to attract others, yet broadly enough to include the opinions, skills, and powers of all the group members.

The following anecdote shows how this works:

> *A collaborative initiator in a rural part of Pennsylvania wanted to gather people together in a joint effort. As he explained, "I want to make sure that we don't spend money twice for the same product!"*
>
> *He believed the answer to the problem was centralized services. However, as the collaboration worked together, the group realized the issue was access to services. So they built a partnership around transportation—including maintenance and fleet purchasing—leaving the services at their scattered sites. Fortunately, he valued the opinions of his partners in the collaboration.*

Power is important here too. Someone with acknowledged power says, "Let's get going on this." This initiator tends to have a title (board chair, legislator, executive director). When this kind of powerful person initiates a meeting, we attend whether or not we believe strongly in the joint effort. Those initiators without acknowledged powers must be clear about the destination, especially the potential gain for their partners, and carefully plan their approach to possible group members.

Make the Collaboration Work for Everybody

We can create needed rituals by asking group members what they want to feel comfortable. Here's how to proceed:

1. **Ask what rituals are important to each person.** (For instance, members might mention starting time, meeting place, availability of food and drink, management of information, whatever.) Do this in the initial interviews or at the first meetings.

2. **Pool all the requests for rituals.** Then consider which requests best meet the individual needs of the participants while helping to form the group.

3. **Present the rituals to the group.** Build trust by openly discussing the rituals. Decide ways to manage any apparently conflicting rituals.

4. **Distribute copies of the agreed-upon rituals.** Some groups give members special folders for their communications, which in itself is a ritual of managing information.

5. **Periodically review the rituals.** By doing this, we determine which are still valuable and whether to add others.

Choose Potential Members

Initiators unite an appropriate cross section of people for collaboration. Each person brings something for the journey. How do we choose among them so that we have the skills and powers we need? How do we limit our number so that we do not have too much of one thing? How do we make sure that the appropriate minority, grassroots, or end-user groups are represented?

We tend to choose people based on who we know, know about, or know to have access to resources. But, there are many other helpful qualities. Consider these criteria when choosing potential members:

- **Capacity:** The capacity required varies with the scope of the effort. For example, one collaboration of five food-bank members in California built a freezer for food preservation while another collaboration to eliminate family violence had ten groups of twelve people each working simultaneously. In practice, up to fifteen people is ideal for any one group. More than fifteen causes difficulty in scheduling meetings and giving everyone a chance to speak. (See Organize the Effort [Challenge 2C], page 82, for how to organize larger efforts.)

- **Difficulty:** Choosing members is an act of power because they later select strategies and control resources. Given this, initiators may avoid people who oppose them or make them uncomfortable. However, unusual or difficult partners may be beneficial and necessary to a collaboration. In the Tri-County story, Peter wanted to race ahead, while the other partners realized the necessity of long-term planning. Instead of asking Peter to leave, they harnessed his skills. Eventually, Peter became the new leader.

- **Dynamics:** Special relationships outside of the collaboration can affect the dynamics of the group. When close friends, partners, spouses, and so on are in the same group, the work of the group is likely to be discussed at other times. This is neither good nor bad, but we need to be aware of existing relationships when choosing members.

- **Familiarity:** Similarities in purpose, expertise, community, clients, and so on will help the collaboration jell. So will a history of positive working relationships that predate the collaboration. (Community here means a group united by geography, population, practice, religion, business, or other shared characteristic.)

> " *Courage happens when people unite.*
> — *Anonymous* "

> " *Power is eroded when differences are suppressed.*
> — *George Peabody American consultant* "

- **Impact:** The proposed members may be the end users (those most directly affected by the joint effort) or people who have access to them. Participation by end users is essential because they know best what they need, and their involvement helps ensure their long-term ownership of the results.

- **Power:** We choose members because they have the power to achieve results. What powers might be helpful? Connections, expertise, resources, position, persuasion, charisma, visibility, and integrity.

- **Stimulus:** Some key people are "queen bees" who attract workers. Given their positions (as county commissioners, school superintendents, famous personalities, directors of large organizations), queen bees do not have time to remain with the collaboration for long. Their initial presence, however, attracts others who will work hard.

- **Territory:** We tend to invite people from similar disciplines. This is especially true of nonprofits working with nonprofits, businesses with businesses, and so on. Instead, include people from as many different sectors as appropriate.

- **Variety:** Some people can conceptualize and have a high tolerance for process; other members prefer to implement specifics later on. Collaborations need varied skills and powers.

Out of the Mainstream

Successful collaborations need to involve minority, grassroots, and end-user groups. This can be difficult when the initiators are from the mainstream. Such initiators can attract these groups by making personal contact, building relationships, and making sure that participation truly benefits them. Even so, mainstream initiators may have to wait until the collaboration is closer to taking specific actions. Then involving the end users is often easier.

To solicit potential members, we consult key people who know the community and understand the collaboration's effort. We saw this in the Tri-County story: Betty Jackson and Wil Gaston, the initiators of the Tri-County collaboration, consulted Kim Lee, the president of the United Way. Then Betty called Marjorie Bear, the assistant director of County Social Services. Together, these key people drafted a list of possible participants.

> " *. . . morality may perhaps consist solely in the courage of making a choice.*
> — *Leon Blum (1872–1950) Premier of France* "

Invite Participation

We can contact a potential member directly or through someone who knows that person. As we make contacts, we must build trust and support. To do this, some initiators bring everyone to the table at once to discuss the collaboration. Others meet privately with each potential partner and summarize the private meetings at the first group meetings. Either way, we need to disclose and obtain the following information:

- **Possible community benefits** and why they are important.

- **Gains** to the participating organizations and individuals (stated in their language).

- **Powers:** connections, expertise, resources, position, persuasion, charisma, visibility, integrity.

- **Commitments** being suggested (staff, time, expertise, dollars).

- **Dates and times** for a first meeting.

Invite a Variety of Groups

Collaboration means working with every group that can contribute to the vision. Admittedly, the contributions of a variety of groups may be uneven—power is never equal—but each can be vital to success. Yet our first thought is usually to invite the biggest, oldest or richest organizations. They can be very helpful and they are often in the middle of most major activities in the community. But because of this, they are sometimes part of the problem. So choose carefully. Choose those groups that can be part of the solution.

Take Time

Sometimes a special meeting is needed to draw the group members together. Do this if the following is evident: low trust among the potential members; strong competition for resources (not just funding); confusion or lack of knowledge among potential members about each other's organizations; or disagreement among key people about which organizations to involve in the collaboration.

It takes time to resolve these issues. Here's how one group responded:

A collaboration of adult literacy providers wanted to integrate their services with social agencies and educators. Their first meeting was side-railed because participants had so many questions about each other's programs. So the literacy folks organized a one-day workshop to identify overlaps and gaps in services.

> *Haste, haste has no blessing.*
> — *Swahili proverb*

A final word about bringing people together: this challenge requires patience and courage. Patience because several meetings may be necessary to assemble the "right" people; courage because we need to select some people while leaving out others.

Group Complexity—No Easy Way Out

Effective communications makes bringing the right number of people together important. If we have two people, two communication bonds exist: (1) what the first person communicates and the second person receives and (2) what the second person communicates and the first person receives. With three people, six bonds exist:

A rule of thumb for all communication bonds is: $N(N-1)$ = Number of Communication Bonds.

So with three people in our group, we have $3(3-1) = 3(2)$ = 6 communication bonds. With eight people, $8(7) = 56$ bonds. With fifteen people, 210 different bonds!

Nonverbal communications also make a difference. If our verbal message and body language match what is expected in our culture, then the message is reinforced. But if nonverbal expression contradicts verbal language (for example, someone claims to be enthusiastic but sits back with arms folded) we receive a confusing message. Add to this the fact that body language varies from culture to culture (for example, eye contact is friendly in some cultures and rude in others) and the opportunities for miscommunication balloon.

What's the implication? The more people involved, the greater the number of communication bonds; the greater the intensity; and the greater the difficulty of learning about each other, balancing power, having time to speak, scheduling meetings, sending out meeting summaries, creating ownership, being productive, and so on.

Urban and Rural Collaborations—Yes, They Differ

People in rural areas tend to be more receptive to collaborations, perhaps due to a relative lack of resources and a sense of isolation from urban areas. They may also be more receptive because people know each other better and have a history of community effort, such as barn raisings and high school sports. As a result, trust and ritual may be easier to build in rural than in urban areas. However, to confront someone's behavior in an urban collaboration when we won't see them until the next meeting is easier than in a rural collaboration where we also worship together and shop in one another's stores.

Because of the variety of relationships, candid discussions about power and self-interests are riskier for members of a rural collaboration. Choosing members is also more difficult because the population is sparser and people in rural areas quickly know who's in and who's out.

Rural collaborations can resolve this dilemma, in which familiarity has both benefits and drawbacks, by imagining that they are consultants to a group facing these problems of familiarity. This exercise fosters the objectivity necessary to finding the answers appropriate to the community.

Adapted from the work of Sharon Kagan. Used with permission.

**Membership
Roster**

Milestones mark accomplishments. We have begun our journey up the hill. Bringing people together wasn't the easiest thing in the world. Still, we're moving forward; we've come to the first bend in the road. Let's mark that by erecting a milestone—a document that summarizes what we've accomplished. For *envisioning results by working individual-to-individual,* the first milestone is a roster of members who have agreed to be part of our fledgling collaboration.

In erecting the first milestone for the challenge of bringing people together, we realize that we have learned:

- The importance of the initiators' self-awareness, base of power, and ability to present an initial vision that is broad enough to include others.

- How to use nine criteria to choose potential members rather than selecting from the more limited group of "who we know."

- How to invite participation by obtaining and disclosing information that builds trust and support.

- The value of taking time, when needed, to draw the group together.

Refer to the Membership Roster, Appendix C (page 147) for a format that records the essential information about the growing membership: names, addresses, and phone numbers; statements of self-interest; and possible contributions.

As we rest by this first milestone in the hill country, we look up and see that the hill is getting steeper. We'll need a lot of trust as we offer each other a helping hand up the road. So, our next challenge is to enhance trust.

Enhance Trust (Challenge 1B)

An initiator builds trust and creates rituals to bring people together. Usually, an initiator of the collaboration becomes its convener. This works when the person has preferences for both begetting and becoming (see page 32). But those who initiate collaboration and favor begetting (discovering, exploring, creating) may not do as well with becoming (focusing, attending to detail). And becoming is more of what is needed to convene regular meetings of the collaboration.

In the Tri-County story, Betty shows she values begetting when she picks up the phone to call Wil and both are excited about possibilities. Kim values becoming and often helps members focus on issues in the meeting.

The initiator serves the collaboration best by recognizing his or her preferences, using those strengths, and admitting to limitations. Most importantly, the effective initiator acknowledges when the time has come to pass the compass to the convener as the travelers journey up the hill, helping each other along the path.

So this next challenge is about enhancing trust between the initiator, the convener, and the partners. Recognizing that unlike the story, everyone is not open and honest, to enhance trust, the collaboration has to:

- Choose a Convener
- Hold Effective Meetings
- Involve Everyone in the Meetings
- Disclose Self-Interests

Enhance Trust

Choose a Convener

A skilled convener needs good organizing and interpersonal skills, especially the ability to challenge assumptions. Those who travel with this tour guide must see her or him as a capable and neutral person. These skills help the convener establish the trust necessary to reach the destination. The convener helps create the routines (rituals) that make our journey enjoyable and satisfying.

Get Started

Often, at an early meeting, someone says, "Everyone's not represented who should be." Yes, all parties affected by the work of the collaboration need a voice in it. However, the timing of that representation is important. We must beware of getting caught in the "diversity trap"— the belief that we can't go forward because we don't have total representation or our members don't reflect the race, ethnicity, class, or other characteristics of the individuals who will ultimately benefit. Instead, we must continually learn, adding people to our collaboration. Our collaboration is a cloverleaf, always coming back on itself, improving and growing. So let's get started and plan how to add the right people very soon.

We must select the right person as our convener—someone who can be supportive and flexible; facilitate the group's work; assume authority as negotiated with the group; delegate responsibility for specific steps; build conditions by which individual members can influence the whole group; remain rather distant from the content of what we are discussing; and focus on the process (the vision, the actions of group members, and what is needed to move things forward). A successful convener makes the group powerful enough to accomplish its own work, powerful enough to reach its destination.

Not-So-Skilled Conveners

How can we go forward when no one in our group seems to have all the skills of a qualified convener? The answer lies in asking the right questions:

- How can we, together, build a vision that motivates, inspires, and affirms values?

- How can we move forward, be sensitive to conflict, and resolve differences?

- How can we be supportive and flexible?

- How can we facilitate our group's work?

- How can we delegate authority and responsibility for specific tasks?

- How can we build conditions by which members can influence the whole group?

Any convener can ask these questions; a more skilled convener may help the group arrive at the answers as part of its collaborative work; a not-so-skilled convener can make answering the questions the temporary work of the group.

Hold Effective Meetings

Effective meetings are themselves a ritual, marked by such routines as starting and ending times, agendas, or refreshments. Effective meetings are important throughout the life of the collaboration, especially in the beginning. The Tri-County story showed effective meetings in which the partners built trust and familiarity through contact, exchanged important information, envisioned results, created strategies, divided responsibilities, and took action.

Initial collaborative meetings are often enjoyable because we are building relationships, establishing a new context for existing relationships, and exchanging information and ideas. But meetings can go sour when relationships are already established or when no one provides valuable information. Then the group makes no important decisions and the purpose of the meeting is ambiguous.

To avoid this souring ambiguity, we must jointly define much-used terms such as *trust, respect, effectiveness,* or *responsibility.* The following exercise deals with potential ambiguity. Modify it so it's appropriate to the culture of the group:

1. State the term. For example: *trust.*

2. Brainstorm specific behaviors that lead group members to conclude there is poor trust. For example: "People are frequently late for meetings."

3. Brainstorm specific behavior that shows average and excellent trust. For example: "People attend meetings but don't say much." "Other people frequently offer new ideas and also listen well to others."

4. From these lists of behaviors (with negative behaviors inspiring their positive opposites), jointly create a short phrase that defines the term.

When terms are jointly understood, nothing is hidden in ambiguity. Either our meetings are effective (as we have jointly defined effectiveness) or we have something to fix.

Different cultures define effective meetings differently. For one group, starting and ending at a preset time might be criteria for an effective meeting. For another group, making sure that everyone leaves with an increased sense of cohesiveness might be a criterion for an effective meeting; for them, ending "on time" is defined not by the clock but by the quality of the relationships.

> "
> *Consciousness raising is putting a question after an assumption.*
> — *Leonard Hirsch American consultant*
> "

> "
> *You will do foolish things, but do them with enthusiasm.*
> — *Colette (1873–1954) French author*
> "

It's a great satisfaction knowing that for a brief point in time you made a difference.

— Irene Natividad Philippine/American political activist

Involve Everyone in the Meetings

The convener must involve everyone by building relationships, taking action, and providing information. Below are ways to accomplish that involvement. Each method must be adjusted so that it's appropriate to the group. For example, one group's "action agenda" may be a written list of items to be covered, while another group's action agenda may be to eat together and know each other better before discussing work at a future meeting. In either case, shared expectations and open decisions go a long way toward enhancing trust within the group.

Planning:
- State the purpose for the meeting(s).
- Issue materials for participants to read or prepare prior to the meeting.
- Create an action agenda by stating the disposition, responsibility, and time allocation for each item.
- Manage the logistics (date, location, start-stop times, refreshments).

Process:
- Set initial ground rules for participation and decision making.
- Begin and end on time.
- Follow the action agenda (but don't stay on a task just to avoid conflict).
- Get the work done that needs to be done.
- Review what has been accomplished (or not) and understand what happened (or didn't).

People:
- Acknowledge contribution and participation.
- Build in rewards (see page 92).
- Manage critical situations and conflict.
- Follow up with those who did not attend.

Paperwork:
- Keep appropriate records.
- Manage the amount of paper.
- Write meeting summaries.
- Distribute essential information to members and other stakeholders.

Meeting summaries are reports that briefly note who attended, the key issues covered in the meeting, actions taken, who is responsible for each action and by when, all progress, and the main items for the next meeting. Summaries are not minutes, which are a recording of *all* discussion. Since no one reads them, summarize!

Intervene for Effective Meetings

Any group continually improves by modifying its ideas and behaviors through the interaction of its members. While conveners do not control others, they do respond to situations in a way that can strongly influence others. Key here is the ability to intervene at the needed moment with a variety of responses. Conveners' interventions can be:

- **Conceptual:** an overview that pulls together the ideas and trends with which the group has been dealing. ("We've addressed a number of ideas tonight, and all of them seem to be concerned with ways to reach agreement.")

- **Experiential:** an expression of current behavior or a report of personal experience. ("I'm feeling pretty tense over what just happened.")

- **Structural:** a suggestion of planned activities to focus attention on the issues at hand; this may include taking a break. ("We seem bogged down. Let's break into small groups and brainstorm solutions to our problem.")

The convener may direct intervene with the group as a whole, a relationship within the group, or the actions of one member of the group.

Because these interventions increase group effectiveness, they also affect the trust level. Sometimes an intervention works; sometimes it doesn't. If an intervention fails, try another. Remember, the one guarantee of failure is to let the group simply plod on without doing anything!

Based on The Critical Incident In Growth Groups *by Arthur M. Cohen and R. Douglas Smith. Used with permission.*

Emphasize the First Meetings

Pay special attention to the first few meetings; proceed slowly, and make the agenda for the first meeting clear with established ground rules. (Of course, the group will later develop these ground rules in more lasting structures, roles, and procedures.)

Consider the following questions for the first agenda:

- Why was the meeting called and who called it?

- What do people think the collaboration might accomplish? In other words, what are the expected community benefits and individual self-interests?

- What are the pros and cons of collaboration?

- Who is not present who might have something to contribute?

Questions to consider for ground rules:

- What are the roles of the members and the convener, and who do they represent?

- What is our time frame for working?

- How will we handle information: data gathering, record keeping, confidentiality, publicity?

- How will communications be managed? In other words, who will see what at what times?

- What, if any, compensation will members receive (fees, expenses)?

- What do we do to get started?

- How will we make decisions?

66

God protect me from self-interest masquerading as moral principle.

— Mark Twain (1835–1910) American humorist and author

99

Disclose Self-Interests

Building mutual respect, understanding, and trust is crucial in this first stage of collaboration. We accomplish this when we acknowledge how the collaboration serves our self-interests as well as the goals of our home base organizations.

In an early Tri-County meeting, both Wil and Marjorie acknowledged their self-interests. In fact, each Tri-County member shared his or her reasons for working in collaboration, and as their discussion exposed personal agendas, their assumptions disappeared. Self-interests must remain in the forefront throughout the life of the collaboration, and effective collaborations renegotiate them as members and self-interests change.

To disclose self-interests, we discuss the areas important to us, including our customs, languages, and preferences. One way to discuss self-interest is for the convener to ask each person to address the following five items, both for what each individual personally needs and what the person believes his or her organization wants:

- **Culture:** Cultural differences, inherent in different ethnic groups, also exist between businesses, government, education, and nonprofits. Cultural differences also extend to organizations, professions, and different parts of the country. The collaboration must discuss its cultural expectations and what will satisfy members.

- **Gain:** Each organization and individual represented in the collaboration stands to gain something from being there: money, prestige, contacts, advancement, goodwill, and so on. A simple question, "Why are you here?" answered by each member from both a personal and organizational perspective goes a long way toward establishing trust.

- **Diversity:** The image of the melting pot is no longer accurate. Today, people seek acceptance of their differences. For some, diversity is recognition of skin color, ethnic background, or sexual preference. Others consider diversity to be acceptance of their style (begetting, becoming, being, or bequeathing) while still others want acknowledgment of how their family situation influences their ability to contribute. Individuals must define *diversity;* the group must define *acceptance.*

- **Perception:** The group must work together to come up with joint definitions of how to perceive actions and other aspects of the collaboration. For example, someone does not show up for the meeting. One interpretation is that the person is detained, and the response is "I'm concerned." Another interpretation is that the person is forgetful, and the response is "Not trustworthy." To avoid judgments when dealing with ambiguous terms or situations, we must find common definitions.

66

You cannot shake hands with a clenched fist.

— Indira Gandhi (1917–1984) Prime Minister of India

99

- **Power:** Members need to disclose what power they bring the group. Some people hesitate to admit to their expertise, wealth, connections, and so on; some refuse to share what they hope to obtain from the power of others. Remember, power is always present and never equal. We must disclose the power that exists and is sought and use group wisdom and convener skills to make sure that we use these powers wisely.

To disclose self-interests, make their discussion an official part of a meeting. Document the discussion in a meeting summary, and set specific times to review self-interests at later stages.

◆ ◆ ◆

The milestone for the challenge of enhancing trust is meeting summaries that clarify the role of the convener, state how everyone is involved, and summarize decisions made and achievements to date. Refer to the Meeting Agenda and Summary in Appendix C (page 149) for a form to record this information.

In erecting this second milestone, we realize we have learned how trust and ritual are the foundation for:

- Choosing a neutral convener who is supportive and flexible with good organizing and interpersonal skills.

- Holding effective meetings that build relationships, provide valuable information, and lead to making important decisions.

- Involving everyone in the meetings by attending to planning, process, people, and paperwork.

- Disclosing individual and organizational self-interests.

Well, we're higher up the hill now. As we've climbed, we've paused to share why we came on this journey. And our sharing has developed trust and helped us realize that our goals may differ.

What lies around the next bend? Confirming our vision. *#3 Our vision*

Meeting Agenda and Summary

steps
1) why we are doing this
2) develop trust + realize goals may differ
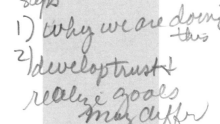

Confirm Our Vision (Challenge 1C)

As we continue our journey, we need to shape our diverse opinions about communal benefits and separate self-interests into a specific vision. Then we can move in one direction, together.

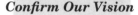

Confirm Our Vision

The Tri-County group agreed early on that they needed a vision statement so everyone would share a sense of purpose. Three weeks later, the participants brainstormed their long-term destination in the form of a vision statement. Then two collaborative partners volunteered to write the statement, which the whole group refined.

Without a vision statement, separate self-interests can override collaborative interests: I try to get my self-interests met and you do the same. With a common vision, however, we apply our power and subordinate our separate self-interests to the larger purpose.

To complete this challenge, we:

Understand Vision Statements

Write a Vision Statement

Capture the Focus

Understand Vision Statements

A shared vision is essential to enhancing trust. The vision statement tells everyone where we are going. It informs everything we do and generates excitement for all parties. Here are two examples:

- *All youth in our city will have, as their birthright, opportunities through education and employment at both the secondary and post-secondary levels to empower them to shape their own future.*

- *Our mission is to expand the role, enhance the status, and increase the ability of women to gain more control over life choices and achieve equal status in business and government.*

> ### Collaboration or Resuscitation?
>
> **Don't collaborate solely to rescue member organizations from financial trouble. To call such a rescue operation a collaboration misleads people. An organization that wants to collaborate to obtain money probably does not have a vision of how collaboration benefits the community. Save anything worth saving; help an agency secure funds if it serves the community well. But don't consider a rescue operation to be a collaboration.**

Let's look at two types of vision statements: *broad change* and *practical efforts.** Broad change mobilizes interest and keeps the collaboration from focusing too narrowly or from launching mini-projects of marginal gain. However, achieving broad change is more difficult than accomplishing practical efforts. Moreover, members who need concrete results to sustain their interest find practical efforts appealing. We can achieve these relatively early, and this type of vision guides day-to-day activities. But practical efforts may not be broad enough to sustain the interests of the greater community or those with resources. A vision that balances broad change and practical efforts is ideal.

Our vision statement should include the following elements:

- **A description of what we will accomplish, as well as where and for whom we will achieve our vision.** The vision must be an exciting destination worth "going for"; right now, our statement will not include how we will achieve our results.

- **An account of the scope of work.** The vision statement must indicate how big, how many, how much.

- **A statement of unique purpose.** The vision statement must differ from the missions of member organizations.

- **Clarity.** The vision statement must be easy to understand, yet go beyond trite phrases.

Vision focuses on possibilities, not problems. A vision statement leads us toward desired results, generating energy and motivation. With a clear vision, we will be better prepared to know what actions to take.

* *From the work of Sharon Kagan. Used with permission.*

Write a Vision Statement

Words are important in our vision statement because all the collaborative members and the people in their home organizations will read them. But since collaboration is an ongoing journey in which we will return to earlier steps with greater expansion and clarity, we must avoid striving for the "perfect" words. We spend time on words because they give us direction, but not so much time that they limit progress. We strive for consensus; everyone agrees to move forward, even if everyone doesn't accept all the words in the vision statement.

To write a vision statement, brainstorm and list important phrases or words that begin to describe the vision. Then agree on the most important factors, and begin to refine the vision statement. Next, ask a subgroup to take responsibility for drafting the statement. At a later meeting, the entire group modifies and ratifies the document. Depending on the extent of our comments, the subgroup may need to meet again. In refining the vision, we realize that the discussion—even the conflict—is more important than the statement itself.

Some conflict in wording is inevitable and actually healthy, because the collaboration sorts out values and attaches meaning to phrases the members have tossed around. But beware of conflicts that arise from a perceived threat to some agency or person. If this type of conflict happens, the convener must emphasize that the group is not yet making operational decisions.

The Children's Fire

A vision statement serves a purpose similar to the Native Americans' ritual of the "children's fire." The community sits around the fire and debates what needs to be done and how best to do it. The elders have the task of repeatedly asking: "How will what you say serve the children to the seventh generation?" Those present argue the validity of opinions and preferences only as these serve the community.

Data Gathering—@#$%&*#$ (Expletive Deleted)

We are ready to write our vision statement and someone says, "We have to gather data about needs. People won't listen to us if we can't demonstrate need." Yes, we need background information to show that we know what we are talking about. But we don't need a lot. And we need to remember the following:

1. Many organizations gather data, a lot of data.

2. We usually don't need to gather new data—we just need to breathe life into existing data and models.

3. Data gathering is used to build relationships and ownership for our effort. This is a strategy. Who we ask for information and how we present the data to our constituencies is just as important as the information itself.

Before adopting a vision statement, collaborations usually work through a series of debates. Some groups have taken as much as two years to agree on a vision. If vested interests are deep-seated, then our emerging collaboration should pick a small, noncontroversial vision, expanding to a more comprehensive vision when we have greater experience. Whatever our statement, we need to begin with something that will lead to success.

Capture the Focus

The Tri-County partners produced both a vision statement and a focus statement. The latter was a single sentence: *Our focus: Agencies working together to keep families together.* This succinct statement became the group's rallying point; it captured the intent of the vision and the imagination of the group.

Because it is brief, clear, and memorable, the focus statement communicates our purpose to people outside our collaboration more readily than the vision statement. The focus statement often becomes a slogan. Following are two examples:

Vision: *All youth in our city will have, as their birthright, opportunities through education and employment at both the secondary and post-secondary levels that will empower them to shape their own future.*

Focus: *Our youth will be ready for the workplace of tomorrow.*

Vision: *Our mission is to expand the role, enhance the status, and increase the ability of women to gain more control over life choices and achieve equal status in business and government.*

Focus: *Women will be equal anywhere and everywhere.*

While writing a focus statement, our collaboration becomes an advertising agency! In this age of the fifteen-second sound-byte, we must communicate essence in an easy-to-grasp phrase. (See Create Visibility, page 119.) To arrive at this focus, brainstorm phrases and then agree on one phrase that communicates the heart of the vision.

> **"**
> *'How' is a destroyer of vision.*
> — *Don Coyhis Founder, White Bison, Inc.*
> **"**

> **"**
> *Imagination is the highest kite one can fly.*
> — *Lauren Bacall*
> **"**

Vision and Focus Statements

◆ ◆ ◆

The milestone for the challenge of confirming our vision is a vision statement that includes a succinct focus. Refer to Vision and Focus Statements in Appendix C (page 151) for a guide to creating these statements. This record aids in achieving support from key stakeholders.

In erecting the third milestone, we have learned how trust and ritual underlie:

- Understanding that vision statements are the basis for everything we do and generate excitement for everyone involved.

- Creating a vision statement using a process that involves everyone, acknowledges that conflict is healthy, yet expedites the writing of the actual statement.

- Capturing the focus of the vision in a brief and memorable phrase that readily communicates the purpose of the collaboration.

Here we are, still climbing that hill! We've established trust and selected someone to call us together. Now we look to the crest of the hill and see that someone holds high a flag. On this flag is our focus statement, the rallying cry that leads us onward.

What must we do next? Specify the results we want to achieve.

Specify Desired Results (Challenge 1D)

Our next challenge is to specify the results we want to achieve. Our vision statement points out where we are headed; our focus statement leads us forward. The statement of desired results is a declaration of the accomplishments we want to make that contribute to the realization of our vision and focus. The more specific the desired results, the better we'll know how we are progressing. They remind us to stop, look around, decide if we're succeeding, and continue on our course or correct it if needed. The more specific our desired results, the more we can trust that we will arrive at our destination—together.

Of course, the desired results will evolve and the final destination may be unforeseeable now. Still, we focus on destination when we:

Define Desired Results

Think Strategically

Take Strategic Action

Specify Desired Results

Define Desired Results

To incorporate the desires of many constituencies and to sustain our collaboration over time, desired results must be long-term. They must also be short-term enough to produce achievements that sustain enthusiasm. These desired results are, of course, community benefits and separate self-interests.

Desired results must be concrete, attainable, and measurable—at least to a degree. That way, our collaboration and our constituents will know *what* we are trying to achieve and *when* our attempt is successful. The words we use must represent positive outcomes, not problem reduction, because when language focuses on problems, problems remain in the forefront. However, when language focuses on achievements, achievements stay uppermost.

Let's return to our story. When the Tri-County collaborative moved into outlining specific desired results and strategies, a small group agreed to refine the ideas and mail out the draft statements so everyone could review them before the group met again. The group came up with an impressive list of hoped-for results and strategies, including:

> *I know why there are so many people who love chopping wood. In this activity one immediately sees the results.*
>
> —Albert Einstein

- *Shorter-term*
  - *Provide up to seven days lodging for every homeless person and his or her family in the Tri-County area.*
  - *Immediate access to the closest available bed for each homeless person.*

- *Longer-term*
  - *Incidence of homelessness reduced by 30 percent during the next eight years.*
  - *Public consciousness raised about what being a member of this community means as measured by increased volunteer support at shelters and food shelves.*

Results: The Buck Stops Here

Specifying desired results is risky because members of a collaboration begin to hold themselves accountable. If they are unsuccessful, they find little place to hide. So some of us are reluctant to get specific. Nevertheless, if people both inside and outside the collaboration know that the collaboration is succeeding, then obtaining and sustaining support and resources will be easier.

Let's remember that desired results differ for every collaboration, they must be specific, and are developed more fully as we move along. Clear-cut objectives build a favorable social and political climate in which constituents see our work as cost-effective and as an improvement to current efforts. This sustains excitement about our collaboration and builds support in the greater community.

 **Getting the Most for Your Money**

Specifying desired results is not easy. To make them appeal to the greatest number of people, desired results must show:

- **Relative Advantage.** Are the desired results better than the status quo? Will people perceive them as better? (If not, they will not be adopted quickly, if at all.)

- **Compatibility.** How do the desired results fit with people's past experiences and present needs and values? (If the results don't fit, people will believe too much change is required of them.)

- **Low Complexity.** How difficult are the desired results to understand and apply? (The more difficult, the slower the adoption process.)

- **Trialability.** Can people try out the change first? (If our constituencies must commit everything at once, they will be far more cautious about adopting the desired results.)

- **Visibility.** How observable are the desired results? If our constituencies adopt them, can the differences be discerned by others? (If not, the desired results will spread more slowly.)

Adapted from Alan AtKisson "The Innovation Diffusion Game" Context Institute, P.O. Box 11470, Bainbridge Island, WA 98110. Used with permission.

To determine desired results, we brainstorm how we will know when we have achieved our vision. We begin by asking, "What will have happened?" " What will have been created?" "What will have changed?" Working together, we agree on the most important results.

Next, as the Tri-County group did, we ask two or three people to take responsibility for writing the statement of desired results. When the subgroup returns with their document, we modify and ratify it. Depending on the extent of the ensuing group discussion, the subgroup may meet again to reword the document.

Think Strategically*

In this book, *strategy* is amplifying resources and relationships to generate revenue and other support prior to taking action. Here are some examples of strategic actions:

- *An organization used money from one program to augment a second program. The second program qualified for matching federal funds. The matching funds increased the second program's revenues by 50 percent and repaid the first program.*

- *A collaboration member agreed to obtain grants. Three times he contacted foundations solely to learn about each one's mission, but never asked for funding. In the second call, he said he was intrigued by the first conversation; during the third call, he said that previous conversations had helped him conceive a program for which he would like advice. Only on the fourth call did he ask if the foundations would entertain a proposal. By this time, some had lost interest. Others, however, did fund the program, including one foundation which gave $100,000, despite never having funded a collaboration before.*

To amplify revenue and other support, our most effective route is through networks (informal groups of people we count on for prompt and cooperative responses). To influence people's decision-making, we must know people who can influence other people. Thus we create stakeholders: individuals, groups, and organizations with a stake in the objectives of our collaboration.

The larger our vision, the more wisely we must create our stakeholders. We tend to talk to people who already support us, but to pave the way for the collaboration's actions, we must include people who are "persuadable."

> "
> *Any enterprise is built by wise planning, becomes strong through common sense, and profits wonderfully by keeping abreast of the facts.*
> — *Proverbs 24:3–4 The Living Bible*
> "

---

* *Strategic thinking and the steps that follow are adapted from the work of Leonard Hirsch. Used with permission.*

To proceed, list potential stakeholders by asking, "Who really supports our efforts?" "Who opposes our efforts?" "Who can we persuade to help?" Include all possible stakeholders, both inside and outside the collaboration. Rate the stakeholders as F ("For"), A ("Against"), and P ("Persuadable"). Typically, we expend 80 percent of our effort on "Fors"; 15 percent on the "Againsts"; and 5 percent on the "Persuadables." But our energy is better used if we expend 15 percent of our effort on the "Fors"; 5 percent on the "Againsts"; and 80 percent on the "Persuadables."

To determine the sequence of approaching the stakeholders, we rate them from 1 to "n" (1, being the most important stakeholder and n being the number of stakeholders). However, to affect the higher-rated stakeholders, we may need to reach the lower-rated ones first, because they, in turn, might be able to influence the higher-rated stakeholders more successfully than we can.

Take Strategic Action

After naming our stakeholders, we have to anticipate their reactions to our desired results and state how we can tie our agenda to theirs. In other words, we show how our results will help the stakeholders. This strategic action helps increase support for the collaboration's efforts. We redefine our desired results based on these considerations and ask a subgroup to revise the statement of desired results.

> **Sometimes, an effective strategy is to include the agendas of those who oppose us. Remember, our reason for creating a collaboration was to build a greater power base. We build power when we use the energy of others—all others—to achieve our results.**

Having decided who is "For," "Against," and "Persuadable," we plan specific actions to influence each of the key stakeholders, giving most of our effort to the "Persuadables." Make a list of those actions, including who is responsible and when each action should be completed.

The final part of taking strategic action is to begin evaluation. While this book explores evaluation in Evaluate the Results (see page 106), taking strategic action includes elements of evaluation—knowing what we are doing and what we are accomplishing every step of the way. We begin evaluating ourselves now because it generates confidence in our early successes, thus building momentum for the challenges that lie ahead.

◆ ◆ ◆

Desired results and strategies that include the perspectives of key stakeholders are the milestone for this challenge of specifying desired results. Refer to Desired Results and Strategies in Appendix C (page 152) for a checklist of desired results and details on specifying strategies.

Erecting this fourth milestone demonstrates we have learned how trust and ritual are the foundation for:

Desired Results and Strategies

- Defining desired results for both community benefits and separate self-interests that are concrete, attainable and measurable.

- Thinking strategically in ways that amplify revenue and other support prior to taking action.

- Taking strategic action by redefining the desired results in ways that show benefit to the stakeholders.

We've come to the end of Stage 1 and the four challenges of this hill country. Climbing together, we've built individual-to-individual relationships. We've accomplished a great deal because we've trusted one another with our separate and community interests. Together, we've envisioned the destination toward which we are now headed. We're over the crest of the hill; where to next? The marshland. ◆

Stage 2: Empower Ourselves by Working Individual-to-Organization

Slogging Through the Marshland

Here we begin to work individual-to-organization to clarify the relationships that empower us to act. One person cannot empower another. But together we can build the power we need.

To empower ourselves, we need authority to make decisions and take action. We gain this authority through continuous negotiation with our home base organizations. Because no group can ever fully clarify authority, we must act within the ambiguity that is always present. Therefore, to achieve our destination (community benefits and individual self-interests), we must push the outer limits of authority.

At this stage we all need a sense of humor to help us slog through the marshland. The ability to laugh at oneself and laugh with others relieves pressure and allows us to continue our work. Two examples illustrate humor in action:

- *One group devoted the first ten minutes of every meeting to the ritual of "checking-in." Members talked about personal and professional events that had helped and hindered their contribution to the collaboration (this also served as a transition, allowing members to shift focus). The group encouraged jokes and applauded humorous responses.*

- *Another group was graced with a storyteller who managed conflict by telling funny stories: "You know, this reminds me of . . ." People laughed, the tension dissipated, and the group moved from opposition to problem solving.*

> "
> *. . . perhaps one has to be very old before one learns how to be amused rather than shocked.*
>
> — *Pearl S. Buck (1872–1973) American novelist*
> "

While authority and humor are needed at all times, they will be especially helpful as we work individual-to-organization. During this stage, we will encounter four key challenges:

Confirm Organizational Roles

Resolve Conflicts

Organize the Effort

Support the Members

Confirm Organizational Roles (Challenge 2A)

Confirm Organizational Roles

At this point, most home organizations are saying to their representatives, "Enough of this planning. Let's do something." In fact, the tendency is to want to skip the organizational challenges of working individual-to-organization (Stage 2). "I won't be able to come to any more meetings if I can't prove we're getting something done" is a common cry for hurrying on to the action of Stage 3.

But action without authority will surely sink us in the swamps. Our collaboration still needs to:

Document Progress

Obtain Authority within the Home Organization

Secure Letters of Commitment

Clarify Authority within the Collaboration

Document Progress

At the beginning of this stage, we inform each home base organization that so far our *product* is our *process*. If we are to be successful, we must value planning as much as we value doing. To create our collective culture, we then do the following:

- **Affirm process and planning.** We focus on process and planning because they are the basis for everything we do together—our roots.

- **Keep an open mind.** While realizing that some ideas might be wrong, we must also reexamine our basic assumptions about what is right. We're not ready to make decisions yet; we're still in the marshland, exploring alternatives. A sense of humor helps us be open to new possibilities.

- **Recognize that our collaboration will not, at first, save money or time.** In fact, expect the collaboration to take longer to get the job done at first. Consider a "cap" on resources expended. When the cap is reached, take time to evaluate the investment. Eventually the collaboration will accomplish more, with greater speed, quality, and scope than each of our organizations is likely to achieve alone.

Review milestones (the documents we've created thus far) with key people in each organization, and invite their ideas and recommendations. Then distribute a summary document to everyone who needs to know and who is likely to influence the course of action.

> **"**
>
> *To move freely you must be deeply rooted.*
>
> — *Bella Lewitzky*
> *American ballet dancer*
>
> **"**

Obtain Authority Within the Home Organization

By the first summer of the Tri-County collaboration, Betty and Wil had each secured authority to spend up to $2,000, and both had convened staff meetings to discuss the implications of the collaboration. Others had trouble gaining authority, and two members were unable to obtain any authorization.

Being a Responsible Partner

In reviewing the progress of the collaboration, each of our home organizations needs to:

- **Know its mission and desired results.** If our home organization's mission and goals are not clear, now is the time to clarify them.

- **Know its self-interests.** Our home organization must know what return-on-investment it expects from the collaboration.

- **Focus on the communal benefits.** That is, make sure our organization knows why it is collaborating for the long-term.

- **Realize how much time collaboration will take.** Because building mutual respect, understanding, and trust takes time, our home organization must be sure the communal benefit is worth the time investment.

- **Review each member's power, commitment, and capabilities.** Our home organization must be aware of what each member organization brings to the table.

- **Modify the way it operates.** Our home organization will experience the greatest success when it changes its policies and procedures to facilitate collaboration.

Look Before You Leap!

The value of planning is borne out in research and practice. In one test, a facilitator places a model made of interlocking plastic blocks on a table, divides the group into teams, and gives each team the exact number, size, and color of blocks to duplicate the model. The facilitator states three rules: (1) no one can touch the model,   (2) only one person at a time from a team can view the model, and (3) each team can take as much planning time as needed before starting to as-

semble the duplicate model. The facilitator asks each team to simply declare when planning has ended and action begun. The winning team is the one that duplicates the model exactly in the shortest amount of total time.

Invariably, the team with the greater effective planning time wins. What happens looks like this:

Planning ⟶ + Action ⟶ = Winner

Planning ⟶ + Action ⟶ = Loser

Submitted by Peter Mumford, with acknowledgement to the Reed Paper Group Ltd. Reprinted by permission from Canadian Training Methods, *April 1974, pp. 24–25, Patrick Suessmuth and University Associates.*

❝

*Speak silver,
reply gold.*

— *Swahili proverb*

❞

Each member of our collaboration needs to obtain approval to act on behalf of the home base organization. Some of our members have immediate authority; others need the approval of their boss, their boss's boss, or a board of directors. For example:

> *The executive of one organization promised, on the spot, that her agency would provide secretarial support. The mid-level manager from a state office needed time between meetings to obtain approval to host the meetings.*

Of course, the clearer the authority, the more quickly trust builds, power struggles subside, and the right people choose to participate. We secure such authority by asking our bosses and boards questions such as: "What decisions can I make about money, time, and other contributions?" "Can I commit others to participate in joint activities?" "How far can I go in committing the reputation and image of my organization?"

In response to our questions, someone might say: "We'd love to, but we don't have the money," or "It sounds great, but we don't have the staff." At these times, we need to remind our boss or our board that being in a collaboration demands reworking priorities: staffing, budget, timelines. Remember, resources are always available when something seems important enough.

Those of us who represent large agencies may need extended time to obtain approval. We can decrease this time by asking people with greater authority to attend our initial meetings, but sometimes the best we can do is laugh about how long some organizations take to grant approval. Our group must openly plan how to keep such organizations involved during their lengthy approval processes.

Secure Letters of Commitment

❝

*What I wanted
to be when I grew up
was—in charge.*

— *Wilma Vaught
USAF brigadier general*

❞

Since authority is the power and the right to make decisions, take action, and commit resources, each of us needs a letter of commitment from the board or senior officer. The letter should state:

- The organization's commitment to the mission, focus, objectives, and strategies of the collaboration.

- What the organization expects in return for its participation in the collaboration.

- How much time the organization's representative may commit to the collaboration.

- That the organization recognizes that this commitment is part of the representative's job.

- The level of powers that the representative and the organization can commit: connections, expertise, funds, and so on.

These letters of commitment clarify authority and help us pool the powers needed to achieve our destination. Pushing for commitment may scare potential partners. Yet, without the letters, partners may not fully commit. Schedule a meeting to present the letters of commitment and describe each member's authority to act for the collaboration. (If a member cannot secure a letter of commitment, use the meeting to discuss the best timing to secure the commitment necessary for remaining involved.)

Clarify Authority Within the Collaboration

Besides being clear about authority from the home base organization, we have to clarify authority within the collaboration. The following story illustrates why this clarity is necessary:

> *A group dealing with school reform was made up of teachers, administrators, parents, business people, and members from the community. This group was bogged down because twenty-five people made all decisions, from how to infuse new curricula in the school to what food to serve at collaboration-sponsored events. The group was able to move on once it clarified who had authority for specific decisions.*

◆ ◆ ◆

We have begun to empower ourselves by working individual-to-organization. The first challenge in this stage is to confirm organizational roles, and its milestone is letters of commitment. Refer to Letters of Commitment in Appendix C (page 154) for a checklist of major items to be included in the letters.

Letters of Commitment

In erecting this milestone, we have learned that authority and humor underlie our ability to:

- Document progress to acknowledge that, so far, our product is our process.

- Obtain authority within our home organizations to act on behalf of the organization and to rework priorities within the organization that will support the collaboration.

- Secure letters of commitment to detail the authority and pool the powers needed to achieve our destination.

- Clarify authority within the collaboration as to which person or group can make which decisions on behalf of the collaboration.

Here we are. We're ready to set out through the marshes. Let's hope we can avoid capsizing in the murky waters of the swamp!

What lies ahead? The challenge of resolving conflicts.

Resolve Conflicts

Resolve Conflicts (Challenge 2B)

Conflict is inevitable and, actually, highly desirable. Lack of conflict often indicates that issues are buried. But, as sure as there's mud in the marshland, these issues *will* surface, often at the very time we require organizational commitment.

To resolve these conflicts, the collaboration needs to:

> **Expect Conflict**
>
> **Clarify the Issues**
>
> **Create a Conflict Resolution Process**
>
> **Resolve the Unresolvable**

Expect Conflict

Collaborations must form a new culture distinct from the cultures of their home base organizations. Conflicts arise as we create this new culture.

> *In one collaboration, a vocal member kept saying: "We have to call these groups, get input on what we're proposing, and go after funding sources." Two other members argued it was too early to act—they weren't ready. After some discussion, they defined the conflict as a difference in preferences. The first person wanted to move on; the other two wanted to involve everyone in a carefully worded vision statement.*

As individuals and representatives of organizations, travelers bring to their collaboration different preferences, histories, communication patterns, and experiences with decision making. When we don't resolve these differences, we divert time and energy from achieving our destination. For success, conflict cannot be about right and wrong; it must be about differences.

Two Sets of Rules

Life offers two types of games: finite and infinite. Finite games, like football or chess, have set rules that everyone is expected to follow. Infinite games, like marriage or collaboration, have no fixed rules, and what rules there are constantly change. In collaborations, conflict arises about destination and actions because we play infinite games with their changing rules, yet we demand the clear rules of finite games!

Adapted from Finite and Infinite Games *by James P. Carse.*

The Tri-County story reveals that the time schedule was a real source of conflict for Peter. At one of the spring meetings, Marjorie wrote the agenda on the flip chart, and Peter snapped, "That agenda makes no sense. We need to focus on solving problems right now. The shelters are full to the max." Wil responded, "You're out to stonewall us!"

Conflict!

By not allowing conflict, we limit our ability to change. We must build conflict into the life of our group and recognize that we may not, and perhaps should not, resolve some conflicts. Rather, we need to expect, promote, and manage conflict throughout the life of the collaboration.

Clarify the Issues

In our collaboration, we experience many types of conflict. In order to resolve these disagreements, we must clarify the conflict. In the Tri-County story, Wil accused Peter of stonewalling. Fortunately, Betty intervened and said, "Wrong approach! We don't know what Peter's thinking or why." Kim suggested that the group try to find out what everyone was really thinking. Then the group began to discuss the source of the conflict.

The conflict in the story is direct and immediately resolved. Yet often the conflict in the group is masked and takes time to manage. Some people are quiet. Others simply stop coming to meetings. While difficult to do, someone—the initiator, the convener, a member of the group—must find the courage to ask, "What's going on here?" This simple question is often enough for people to start talking and dealing with the conflict.

The chart on the following page shows the typical sources of conflict at this stage and suggests ways to resolve these conflict issues.

Investment in time and discussion to understand and resolve conflict is crucial. Through conflict we gain clarity and build new skills. But most of us find it to be uncomfortable. Therefore, to proceed, define the sources of conflict in the total group and agree to limit the scope of the discussion to the specific conflict at hand. Avoid blaming anyone, but do define the *process* for immediately dealing with the issues.

> "
> *When elephants fight it is the grass that suffers.*
>
> — *Proverb of the Kikuyu people of Africa*
> "

Typical Sources of Conflict

Power struggles

- Members act out of their "shadow" power. (See Sunshine and Shadow Powers, page 34.)

- Personal customs, languages, preferences are not being met.

The wrong people

- People were not well chosen in the beginning. (See Choose Potential Members, page 48, for selection factors.)

Low trust

- The meeting convener lacks the needed skills.

- Meetings are boring and do not accomplish steps.

- Self-interests are not being disclosed.

- Communications are poor.

Vague vision and focus

- The members and organizations frequently call the vision and focus into question.

Incomplete desired results and strategies

- Desired results and strategies are frequently debated, even though they are in writing.

Lack of clear authority

- Home base organizations pressure the collaboration for quick action.
- People attend infrequently, or representation from the organization changes so that new people continually have to be updated.
- Demands are placed on members to work for the collaboration and still fulfill all home base job duties and responsibilities.

How to Resolve the Issues

Address power needs

- Look for underlying issues, such as history of conflict, fearing loss of control or autonomy, need to obtain funding for own operation, and so on.

- Take time to review the customs of the members; define frequently used terms; acknowledge different styles and decide when each will best be used.

Choose new people

- Have the initiator look at her or his reasons for choosing people—be honest!

- Review the selection factors; ask people to choose replacements who bring the needed attributes. (This is difficult to do for risk of offending the person, but crucial.)

Enhance trust

- Choose a new convener; ask the group to take greater shared responsibility for the meetings.

- Review the characteristics of effective meetings and make needed changes; attend to rituals that enhance trust. (See page 55.)

- Disclose the culture, gain, diversity, and perception each person seeks.(See Enhance Trust, page 53.)

- Practice communication skills; review how communications are being managed with the home base organizations.

Strengthen vision and focus

- Review the destination; remember that conflict is often not about wording, but about the scope of effort where some people want specific, readily achieved results while others prefer larger, more complex efforts; set short-term results.

Revise desired results and strategies

- Review desired results for specificity and strategies for attainability; people get "burned-out" when they cannot see concrete accomplishments.

Clarify authority

- Reaffirm the value of planning.

- Ask those with authority in the organization to commit to consistent representation; clarify that a collaborative culture is being built.

- Request that member organizations reduce other duties; formalize those responsibilities in writing

Create a Conflict Resolution Process

We often respond to conflict by complaining to our staff at the home organization. Instead, collaboration members need to risk working out as many disagreements as possible *during* their meetings. How to do this?

- **Revisit the destination.** Ask, "If we want to achieve these results, what must we do about this conflict?" Then determine which issues the collaboration must resolve to do its work.

- **Decide who will facilitate the process for resolving the conflict.** Ask a group member or a third party facilitator, mediator, or arbitrator to lead the group. Or hold an outside session just for those directly involved in the conflict.

- **Separate the conflict from concepts of right and wrong.** Such separation helps the group avoid personalizing the issues, since some people tend to view conflict as a threat to long-held beliefs.

- **Make sure everyone is heard.** Limit those who talk and invite the participation of those who do not. (For example, give everyone the same amount of poker chips, and when they have used up their chips, they cannot speak again.)

- **Don't burn bridges.** Remember, everyone must continue working together during and after the conflict. So create rituals for healing and forgiveness. And don't forget humor.

Resolve the Unresolvable

Sometimes personal enmity and other conflicts cast a long shadow on a collaboration. Because we cannot avoid the conflict, we feel stuck in the marshland, as the following anecdote reveals:

> *In a literacy collaboration, two high-level managers from large agencies would not trust each other. Allegations of secret deals, incompetence, and favoritism raged. The other members felt powerless, and the group developed deep schisms. People waited it out, and eventually one person changed jobs.*

> *Conflict is working through a difference of opinion. Fighting is the avoidance of conflict.*
>
> *— Leonard Hirsch American consultant*

> *If you will not take the risk of offending people, then those people can intimidate you.*
>
> *— George Peabody American consultant*

> *Struggle precedes growth.*
>
> — *Don Coyhis*
> *Founder,*
> *White Bison, Inc.*

To resolve what appears to be an unresolvable problem, consider the following alternatives:

- **Confront the situation outright.** Call a meeting and insist that the warring factions agree on a process to settle the dispute; consider an outside facilitator. If settlement is impossible, create a working agreement and agree to disagree while working together in the collaboration. This can and does work.

- **Confront the situation through people of influence.** Collectively, ask important people (board members, legislators, peers) associated with each of the warring organizations to intervene. This option allows the conflicting parties to fight in another and more appropriate arena than the collaboration.

- **Alert funders and donors to the problem.** While our group might not want to admit that we have a conflict, many funders are knowledgeable enough to know what is really happening. They can influence people who may otherwise seem immune to change. Still, funders give money at their discretion, so weigh carefully the relative advantages and disadvantages of this option.

- **Work without the warring members.** A simple story illustrates this alternative:

  Two teachers initiated a very effective collaboration despite the disapproval of their bosses, who disliked each other. The teachers decided to quietly work together and gather data about their success. When they had enough information, they made joint presentations to their bosses and asked for permission to continue. They also sent word to the local newspaper, which reported the emerging success. The pressure forced the bosses to begin working together. One final word: wisely, the teachers credited their bosses for the success so that all were rewarded for collaborating!

When to Use Outside Help

If the conflict is entrenched, we may need a neutral party (someone with conflict resolution or mediation skills). Use an outside facilitator or mediator when:

- Group leaders are directly involved in the conflict.

- The group is not very skilled in conflict resolution.

- Impartiality is essential.

- Only a few people say there is a conflict and a facilitator is needed to ensure fair representation.

- Cultural equity—giving equal value to different backgrounds—needs to be assured.

- Resources allow hiring a practitioner or seeking a volunteer.

- The group wants instruction in conflict management.

Take care choosing a facilitator because he or she can never be totally removed from the conflict and has the potential to add to the conflict.

◆ ◆ ◆

Document the conflict resolutions as the milestone for this challenge. Refer to Conflict Resolutions in Appendix C (page 155) as a guide and a way to track resolutions.

This milestone demonstrates our learning that authority and humor are the foundation for:

* Expecting conflict and building it into the life of our collaboration.

* Clarifying the issues by recognizing their sources and possible resolutions.

* Creating a conflict resolution process that involves everyone and does not burn bridges.

* Resolving the unresolvable by exploring alternatives to even the most difficult conflict situation.

This pattern of surfacing, resolving and documenting conflict serves the collaboration throughout its life.

When last we looked, the travelers had moved into the murky waters of the marshland. Having reconciled themselves to the inevitability of conflicts, the travelers developed a process for resolving them. Clearly, they are ready to journey onward!

What will they do next? Organize the effort.

Conflict Resolutions

Organize the Effort (Challenge 2C)

Some members of the collaboration may still be pushing to take action, but pulling our boats together is worth the time. Remember, through continued planning, we reduce action time and overall time. The work of one collaboration illustrates this point:

A collaboration wanting to reduce family violence took time to organize the work to be done to achieve its destination. The group saw several areas that it needed to address: government, media, intervention, prevention, business, and religious institutions. The collaboration planned how to have separate teams work simultaneously. In less than one year, each of the teams produced major initiatives.

The example makes it clear that organizing the effort means the collaboration has to:

Form a Structure

Determine Roles

Decide About Staffing

Secure Resources

Form a Structure

Successful collaborations organize themselves as efficiently as possible. Both the process of working together and the results they achieve concern the members. Most partnerships work best when the partners create a structure that helps members manage the extra work that happens when collaborating begins.

Resist creating new organizations complete with board structures and policy books. Instead organize to change the way people exchange information, make decisions, and allocate resources.

Collaborations usually adopt one of two structures: a table or a wheel.* In the table structure, everyone comes together to make the necessary decisions. (Such groups are usually seated around a table.) In the wheel, small groups take more independent action; a group at the hub coordinates information and activities, but the small groups may have little contact with each other.

*"Table"
structure*

*"Wheel"
structure*

* From the work of Sharon Kagan. Used with permission.

However, no structure is pure. The table model may have task forces or subcommittees that act like spokes on the wheel, making recommendations back to the larger group or taking action on behalf of the "table." On the other hand, the spokes on the wheel may each operate like a "table" where all members make all decisions.

In forming structure, determine how *flat* the structure will be. (A flat organization has few people managing others and most people doing the work.) Whether within a table or a wheel structure, collaborations can be:

- **Hierarchical:** One person is in charge of the various groups. Group leaders, in turn, make sure that others who have responsibilities fulfill their duties. This structure, which is more of a pyramid, makes coordination easier, but it may inhibit conflict resolution.

- **Individual-based:** Each person in the group is responsible for a certain aspect of the work. This structure, which is flat, gives each person maximum responsibility. Some collaborations have effectively dispersed leadership with the result that everyone feels involved, useful, and valued. However, more time is required to develop this structure, and coordination can be difficult.

- **Group-centered:** More work is the responsibility of the group, while some activities might remain with individuals. The structure is flat and leadership is dispersed, but, unlike the individual-based structure in which responsibilities are clearly assigned, the group might miss some work, since no one person is in charge.

To form structure, review the vision statement, desired results, and commitments for resources made by member organizations. Ask, What work needs to be done? What kind of groups do we need to form? Who will be in charge of what parts? Then detail the structure by using a model like the table or wheel, drawing the structure, and listing lines of authority for doing the work of the collaboration.

Because our structure is temporary, it must remain flexible—changing with the changing needs of the collaboration; be readily understood by each of us and by our separate organizations; and be discarded when our organizations change the ways they work together. By acknowledging that structure is temporary, we minimize confusion and maximize success.

> **"**
>
> *There can be hope only for a society which acts as one big family, and not as many separate ones.*
>
> — *Anwar al-Sadat (1918–1981) President of Egypt*
>
> **"**

> **"**
>
> *Only in a hut built for the moment can one live without fears.*
>
> — *Kamo no Chomei (1153–1216) Japanese author*
>
> **"**

Determine Roles

We'll look at the roles needed to implement our vision—its services or products—when we discuss action planning later in this handbook. For now, we need to develop clear roles to fit our structure. But we need to avoid quickly dividing up functions and assigning them as roles so we have something to do. Depending on the structure we chose, functions vary. For example, the table structure needs only one meeting facilitator, recorder, and so on. However, in the wheel, each spoke needs its own facilitator, recorder, and so forth. If the group manages some of the work, the collaboration will not need certain individual roles. Whatever the structure, the following functions usually need to be filled and acted on:

> *It is not fair to ask of others what you are not willing to do.*
>
> — *Eleanor Roosevelt*

- **Initiating meetings,** including sending out notices and setting the agenda.

- **Setting up meetings,** including choosing location and providing the refreshments.

- **Leading meetings.** (See Holding Effective Meetings, page 55.)

- **Gatekeeping**—making sure that people are involved and have a role to play.

- **Surfacing conflicts and problems.** (See Resolve Conflicts, page 76.)

- **Recording and distributing** meeting summaries and other documents.

- **Communicating information** to and receiving information from member organizations and the larger community.

- **Managing collaboration logistics,** including setting up a phone, post office box, mail drop, or use of someone's office and staff.

- **Monitoring activities** to achieve the mission and results.

- **Rewarding members** and member organizations.

Assign roles according to the interests and strengths of the collaboration members, because ultimately, people gravitate toward their interest or they drop out. Sometimes, sharing or rotating roles can help ensure that all collaboration members feel involved, useful, and valued.

Add the roles to the organizational drawing and specify when the roles will rotate. This latter action prevents any one person from feeling burdened by taking on just one less exciting function, such as being the recorder.

Decide About Staffing

While most collaborations are staffed voluntarily, they can be difficult to sustain on a purely volunteer basis. The decision to hire staff to fulfill routine functions or implement programs may prove troublesome; while we appreciate the support, we have a hard time finding the dollars to pay them.

Because stability of the collaboration is essential, many collaborations choose to hire staff just to get the partnership started. Successful collaborations tend to have staff, either paid by the collaboration itself or provided by member organizations, because such staff free collaboration members for other roles.

Whether paid by the collaboration itself or provided by the member organizations, the staff members need support, reinforcement, and nurturing. Therefore, clarify their responsibilities and ensure that their role in the collaboration is part of their regular job, not an addition to it.

Staff tend to burn out from their dedication. (Remember, burnout comes not from hard work, but from lack of rewards and recognition.) Staff members deal daily with the ambiguity of diffused leadership and multiple ownership. Having worked hard, they deserve visible credit for a visible role.

Besides staff, consider hiring consultants skilled in collaboration and group process. Able to focus on process, they are unburdened by the issues members may bring to our collaboration, and they do not have a stake in the final results. A consultant can help establish the collaborative effort, refine it, or serve as the facilitator supporting the convener on a regular basis.

Insiders and Outsiders

An outsider can staff a local collaboration. But can an outsider organize local people? Sometimes, yes. Yet in one federally funded project, a government agency sent paid staff into a community to help local people organize a collaboration. The community began to resent that the outsiders were paid well, that they took jobs that community members could have had, and yet did not seem to pull their own weight. The difference between a community organizing and paying staff and paid staff organizing a community is very important.

Adapted from the work of Shelby Andress, Search Institute. Used with permission.

"

*The lands wait
for those who can
discern their rhythms.*

— *Vine Victor Deloria, Jr.
Standing Rock Sioux
author*

"

Secure Resources

Collaborations have two types of resources: *operating* (those used to manage the collaboration's activities) and *project* (those that affect the collaboration's desired results). Resources can be dollars, staff, technology, training, information, contacts—any form of power.

We need an adequate and consistent financial base to support our collaboration. From the onset, our collaboration must have some moneys. Dollars need not be large, perhaps only enough to support meetings and documentation. Yet, to underwrite basic costs, our collaboration has to consider the resources of its members as well as approaches to outside sources.

To create a resource plan, work as a total group or form a subgroup to:

- Review existing resources that members have and can share.

- Look at resources in the community.

- Seek funds and in-kind services to cover what else is needed.

If a subgroup develops the plan, ratify it as a total group.

From working together, we discern that even though resources contributed by members are unequal, we can pool and exchange these resources. Such resource exchange can have a profound effect on the collaboration, because with pooling and exchange we put the existing resources to better use, make them more abundant, and manage them better.

Resource Scarcity—Not True! Not True!

We are told that we're in a time of resource scarcity: government funding is dwindling, corporate support is diminishing, and foundation philanthropy is leveling off. This is all true—and it is not.

We are really in a time of resource abundance. Private wealth is greater than ever before; people and organizations give generously. So what explains the difficulty of getting resources? Selectivity. Government agencies increase their requirements; foundations give less for general grants and more to focused requests; individuals are more circumspect; corporations give increasingly in their self-interests; nonprofits hold on to their existing resources. The resources are there—they just are not where they used to be and are not accessible in the same ways that they once were.

Thus, we can no longer afford to think that because what we have to offer is badly needed, others should simply support the effort. We must know who already supports us; determine who can be persuaded; understand their self-interests; and use their language to explain our efforts. (See Think Strategically, page 67.)

We cannot afford the "poor me" attitude that "they" are not supporting us. The resources are there—the question is only how to access them and how to share them. This is the power of collaboration!

◆ ◆ ◆

Documenting the appropriate structure is the milestone for this challenge of organizing the effort. Refer to Collaboration Structure in Appendix C (page 157) for guides to selecting a structure and level of authority, defining roles, and securing resources.

In erecting this milestone we have learned that authority and humor underlie:

- Forming a structure to organize ourselves as efficiently as possible and deciding how flat the structure will be.

- Determining roles that fulfill key functions in the collaboration.

- Deciding about staffing, how to pay for staff, and how to support them.

- The importance of resources for both operations and projects.

Our journey continues and becomes even more invigorating and challenging! After resolving our conflict over destination, power, and roles, we are now working together. This marshland hasn't defeated us!

What next? Support the members of our collaboration.

Collaboration Structure

Support the Members (Challenge 2D)

Support the Members

To go forward, collaboration members want to know they are supported. This empowers them to take action. To feel support, they need to:

Establish a Decision-Making Protocol

Create a Communications Plan

Reward Members in the Collaboration

Reward Other People

Establish a Decision-Making Protocol

Let's return to our Tri-County story for a brief update: In one of their summer meetings, the group talked about how to make decisions. The meeting went overtime, and tempers ran hot, then cold, then just plain tired. But finally, the partners agreed to the types of decisions they had to make, who would make these decisions, and how much authority each member had. In other words, the group established a decision-making protocol. Our collaboration needs one too. And so do our home base organizations.

A protocol is a written record of our agreements on who can make decisions and what type of decisions can be made. To set up a protocol, first review structure and roles (see pages 82–84). Next, decide which style of decision making will be granted to each of the groups and roles in the structure. Then have a subgroup draft a document that details the types of decisions, who makes these decisions, and what level of decision each person or group can make in a given situation. Last, review the document, modify it, and ratify it. This is all time-consuming, but remember, people are most free to move ahead when they know their limits because they feel responsible for achieving the desired results.

We feel empowered when we understand how we make decisions. Let's look at five styles of decision making appropriate to any decision maker—individual or group—in any situation:

- **Autonomous:** Informing only those who need to know, we make the decision. We do not consult others because the decision is unimportant to them, has no impact on the work of others, or needs only us to implement it.

- **Consultative:** We inform others we will make the decision because we want or need their advice or information or the decision requires support from implementers, from those whose work will be affected, or from those who may be barriers.

> *If someone tells you he is going to make a 'realistic decision,' you immediately understand that he has resolved to do something bad.*
>
> — Mary McCarthy
> American novelist

- **Consensus:** To find common ground, we probe the issues until everyone's opinions are understood, especially opposing opinions. We do this because the decision will impact those who will implement or be affected by it, require the commitment of those affected by it, or we have trust and open communication. We close discussion with agreement on how to proceed.

- **Democratic:** We discuss the options sufficiently so that people understand the consequences of the majority vote. We do this because we want to know what different people think of various options; the decision affects the work of others; we are willing to have winners and losers; or we don't have time for consensus building, but we nevertheless want the group to make a decision. Here we establish the ground rule that the losers support the decision, even though it was not their choice. Then we vote and count.

- **Delegated:** We present the situation and clarify expectations and responsibilities for making and implementing the decision. We do this because the decision impacts the work of others; others possess necessary knowledge, skills, experience, and resources; or others know the limits of the situation. When delegating, we must clarify any constraints on the authority to act and set a time for reporting back to the group.

By choosing the best styles for decision making, our collaboration achieves a balance of ownership and productivity. We achieve the greatest ownership when everyone is aware of all the information and participates in all decisions. However, group ownership can limit power and productivity.

Productivity can be greater when the collaboration empowers individuals and small groups to act unilaterally or in consultation. Why? Because they can get on with the work without having to wait for our entire group to make a decision. Productivity through separate powers, however, limits group ownership.

Collaboration can offer members full responsibility to achieve the change they want by specifying what is expected and by setting the boundaries within which the individual members can operate. To do this, groups need to compromise. Therefore, the participating organizations must give their representatives latitude to work out agreements. Given these various decision-making styles, collaborative members need patience as they consciously work out the balance between limits and independent actions.

> 66
>
> *We must try to trust one another. Stay and cooperate.*
>
> *— Jomo Kenyatta (1891–1978) President of the Republic of Kenya*
>
> 99

"

*All races need to
communicate with each
other and a good way
to start is with a smile
and a blessing.
It is important to
understand each others'
customs so that neither
are blamed mistakenly.*

— *Princess Pale Moon
Cherokee/Ojibwa
foundation executive*

"

Create a Communications Plan

In their meeting on decision making, the Tri-County collaborative partners reviewed the communication plans that a team was developing to make sure that the team would clearly convey the decision-making process. They knew that clear communications would hold their collaboration together and support the members. As the story shows, open communications build mutual respect, understanding, and trust.

To build effective communications, establish informal and formal communication links and communicate openly and frequently.

Informal communications: We handle these at meetings as we share information with one another and as we report data back to our respective organizations. During these informal times, we can establish more personal connections and thus improve communications. Above all, we must teach ourselves to *listen* to each other as we talk with each other. (See Communications—Say What? page 91.) Humor also helps us be open to one another.

Formal and inter-organizational communications: These require time and effort to produce and distribute documentation. They also require an advocate or small group to promote conversation among all and help avoid disagreements that devalue some. Formal communications go a long way to accomplish:

- Thorough involvement in decision making. We acknowledge multiple layers of decision making so that every level within each participating organization is involved and key decision makers participate.

- An understanding of the collaborative structure. We create by-laws (or some form of written agreement on structure and roles) and distribute them to everyone.

- Statements of commitment. Each organization provides written agreements to the collaboration on the use of resources such as consistent representation by the most appropriate person, staff and office space, and contribution of funds.

To set up this formal communication:

- List the key people in each home base organization who are to receive communications and or participate in decision making.

- Outline who will receive specific communications, when they will receive them, who will be asked for feedback, and how to obtain their feedback.

- Decide who in the collaboration will have responsibility for making sure that two-way communication happens with these key people in each home organization.

- Set up communications within the collaboration so all members are informed.

- Add this role to the structure diagram.

Communications—Say What?

Whether communications are formal or informal, communication skills are essential. Practice the following skills:

Behavior Description: Describe specific, observable behavior without inferring anything about motivations, attitudes, or personality traits and without judging whether the behavior is good or bad.

1. *Describing:* Jan came to the meeting thirty minutes late.

2. *Inferring:* Jan is very busy. She likely had a previous appointment.

3. *Judging: Jan is rude. She doesn't care about others.*

Behavior descriptions build healthier working relationships because they help us make conclusions based on observable evidence rather than feelings of fear, affection, irritation, or insecurity.

Paraphrase: In paraphrasing, we state in our own words what we understood the other person to say. The other person acknowledges the accuracy of the paraphrase or speaks to any misunderstandings:

Fran: Kelly should never have joined this group.

Tim: You mean she doesn't like our direction or doesn't like our meetings.

Fran: Not at all. I mean she is already so involved in this effort that she doesn't seem to have enough time for friends and family.

Tim: Oh. Since she is already doing so much in this area, she should take more time for herself.

Fran: Right! A little time for herself will be healthier in the long run.

Paraphrase draws out the speaker, helps expand the speaker's intent, and allows everyone to understand the speaker's meaning.

Feelings Description: While we express emotions in body language, in actions, and in words, a specific expression may signify different emotions (a blush may indicate pleasure, embarrassment, annoyance).

Reporting each person's inner state can build understanding. To do this, name the feeling ("I feel angry") or express a simile (" I feel like a squashed bug") or express an action ("I wish I could just walk out of here"). Of course, we sometimes convey contradictory messages: A person states anger yet smiles. The clearest communication occurs when the spoken expression matches the body language.

Perception Check: We all think we know what the other person is feeling: "Your arms are crossed, you have a scowl on your face; obviously you're angry." But such conclusions may lead to misunderstanding. A perception check allows us to test whether we have accurately decoded the other person's feelings. To do this, transform the other person's expression into a tentative description of feelings. For example: "Am I right that you feel disappointed because no one commented on your suggestion?" Or, "I get the impression you are angry with me. Are you?" A perception check describes the other's feelings without expressing approval or disapproval. We merely convey, "This is how I understand your feelings. Have I hit the bull's-eye?"

Feedback: Feedback helps others consider their behavior. Useful feedback describes rather than evaluates; is specific rather than general; notes behavior the receiver can do something about; is timed well; provides an example of clear communication; and is solicited rather than imposed.

Reward Members in the Collaboration

Let's look at the Tri-County story again. After agreeing on types of decisions and reviewing their plans for communications, the group spent a few minutes talking about what each person needed in order to feel rewarded. The group had worked long and hard, and the members needed to reward one another.

Rewards are actually easy to uncover and deliver. Yet, unlike the Tri-County collaboration, most groups devote no time to rewarding members and stakeholders. But to feel involved, useful, and important, collaboration members must know they are doing a good job; they need to receive rewards for all their time and effort.

Give rewards for work done, milestones accomplished, and results achieved. For some people, a reward is just having their ideas heard or having their contribution recognized; for others, a reward is an attitude, like respect. For still others, a reward is social time with partners away from the collaborative work. The only way to find out what members need for rewards is to ask them. To achieve our destination with grace and goodwill, we must discuss the importance of rewards and build the norm in the group for rewarding people freely and frequently.

> *The convener of one collaboration asked each member to state what he or she needed to feel rewarded. The convener listed all items and grouped them by similar types. Members then brainstormed how the rewards could be delivered and how each member would know when he or she had indeed been rewarded.*

Reward Other People

Collaboration members operate in three cultures: the collaboration, the home base organization, and the larger community. Ideally, the three cultures would reward each other. In reality, the collaboration needs to reward the other two and ask for what it wants from them.

Service is what life is all about.

— *Marian Wright Edelman*
President, Children's Defense Fund

Rewards—Double the Return on Investment

Directly rewarding someone is great. But when we reward someone *indirectly*, both of us gain. If an employee excels, send a message of a job well done to the entire staff. When a member of the collaboration succeeds, let his or her home base organization know, as well as all members of our collaboration.

Indirect rewards increase our own credibility because they increase the recipient's credibility with others and enrich the entire group. Indirect rewards increase reputation—the reputation of the person being rewarded and of the group as a whole.

Adapted from the work of Leonard Hirsch. Used with permission.

Staff—especially the boss—in the home base organization need to be fittingly recognized for supporting the collaboration. Also, the collaboration must reward key leaders, such as county commissioners and school board members, who have supported the group. In both cases, the rewards must fit the recipient's culture.

At the same time, we want to be rewarded by the other two cultures. So we need to be clear about what we want and state how we will know when we receive these rewards. The executive director of the home base organization may occasionally say "way to go" to the organization's representative, but regularly the executive must let the rest of the organization know what is being accomplished and what role the member is playing in achieving results. Similarly, commissioners and board members can make sure the minutes declare what the collaboration is achieving, but we will likely have to ask for this.

We must go beyond our habit of conducting collaboration business. We must regularly stop and ask what has been accomplished, ask for praise, and thank everyone.

◆ ◆ ◆

To fall into habit is to begin to cease to be.

— *Miguel de Unamuno (1864–1936) Spanish philosopher*

The milestone for supporting the members of collaboration is a decision-making protocol and communication plan that includes rewards. Refer to Decision-Making Protocol and Communication Plan in Appendix C (page 159) for a guide.

This milestone demonstrates we have learned that authority and humor are the foundation for:

- Establishing a decision-making protocol that incorporates various styles of decision making.

- The importance of a communications plan for informal, formal, and inter-organizational communications.

- Rewarding members in the collaboration in ways that suit each person.

- Rewarding other people in the home base organization and in the larger community.

Decision-Making Protocol and Communications Plan

We're at the end of Stage 2. We've built the individual-to-organization relationships, and our work—empowering ourselves to act—is well along the way. An increased sense of success surrounds us as we have accomplished more milestones: commitment letters, conflict resolutions, collaboration structure, communication plan. The marshland did not capture or capsize us; we can journey on to the next stage of creating, sustaining, and enjoying collaboration. ◆

Stage 3: Ensure Success by Working Organization-to-Organization

Reaping What We've Sown in the Fertile Plains

We journey now onto the fertile plains of Stage 3. Here, traveling is easier. We begin to reap the benefits of all our experience in the first two stages. We have traveled far to reach a place where our work can build a better community. All this work can be more readily accomplished because we've learned one another's strengths, how to organize ourselves effectively, and how to best use our resources.

Now is the time for us to do the work we envisioned. We work organization-to-organization to ensure the successful results the collaboration seeks. This calls for *output* and *action* between organizations as well as from our collaboration.

What is output? The quantity, quality, and rate of production. The combined energy and resources of all the participating organizations now increase our overall output.

What is action? The exertion of power, the implementation of our vision. To implement our vision, more people at all levels will be involved in our collaboration from now on.

While output and action are always part of the collaborative effort, they are crucial to the four key challenges we face as we work organization-to-organization to ensure success. In facing these challenges, we learn how to:

Manage the Work

Create Joint Systems

Evaluate the Results

Renew the Effort

> *Just go out there and do what you've got to do.*
>
> — *Martina Navratilova*
> *Czech/American*
> *tennis champion*

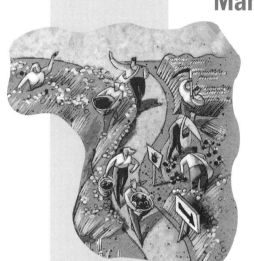

Manage the Work

"

*If you have a
lot of things to do,
get the nap out of
the way first.*

—*An eight year-old*

"

Manage the Work (Challenge 3A)

What did the Tri-County partners do as they came upon the fertile plains? The resource team coordinated volunteers, wrote and received a small grant, and collected information about foundations interested in collaborative approaches to sheltering the homeless. Meanwhile, the planning team identified and priced computer hardware and software that would put the shelters "on line." The groups made decisions quickly; they knew what they were about.

If we are to be as successful as the Tri-County group and achieve both output and action, our collaboration will have to:

> **Review the Vision and Desired Results**
>
> **Lay Out an Action Plan**
>
> **Create Accountability Standards**
>
> **Build Collaborative Work Habits**

Review the Vision and Desired Results

As we begin this work, we need to confirm our destination. In other words, is our initial vision still appropriate? Previously, we tried to ensure that the end user was involved in creating the vision. We also specified desired results and strategies. Now, our collaboration must get specific about the communal benefits. To do this we:

- **Include end users.** Make sure end users are represented in the collaboration. If consumers were reluctant to participate in the earlier stages of "abstract" discussions, include them now, because discussions are concrete and affect them directly.

  In a service collaboration for drug-addicted young mothers, the clients, therapists, public health nurses, and child-care workers were asked to list all things needed to provide enhanced and coordinated services. In a literacy collaboration, adult students were asked to list the barriers to attending classes.

- **Consult existing research.** Look for research on community needs and resources everywhere: police departments, colleges and universities, school districts, private research groups and foundations, libraries, newspapers, businesses, business associations, and state, county, and local government agencies. Computers link these groups to yet other data bases. Most research sources willingly share information and are, in fact, hungry for audiences to use the work they do.

- **Conduct surveys.** Survey community sources and end users if absolutely necessary, but resist recreating what already exists and avoiding action by seeking yet more data. With information in hand, winnow to the nitty-gritty. Do we need to do extensive analysis of data and call in outside experts? Probably not. We know the results we want and why we need them. Revise these desired results as necessary.

Lay Out an Action Plan

After ensuring that the needs of end users are included, develop action plans. This work (and time) vary greatly depending on the collaboration's specific vision and desired results, but here are some principles to include:

- **Be Specific.** State what actions to take. Vague expectations can lead the effort away from the desired results. A subgroup, which might work more quickly, can make detailed recommendations to the total group.

- **Set Responsibilities.** Introducing new services or products requires all members of the collaboration to determine implementation roles, responsibilities, accountabilities and completion dates. Make sure that the implementers are thoroughly involved so they know what they are to do and can help make the decisions that affect them. Actual job descriptions might help, especially when the job as a member of the collaboration differs from the job in the home base organization.

- **Produce a budget.** Show expenses and revenue (both dollars and in-kind support). A subgroup can be efficient here; the total group reviews and ratifies.

- **Communicate with all appropriate people.** Use the communication plan to determine who these people are and what they need to receive.

Sometimes, we need to start small because both the collaboration and those who support it need to see success. The decision to start small is often a good one, since a small venture offers quicker successes and easier access to learning opportunities. Smaller tasks also let the group "practice" before tackling something bigger or riskier. The following stories illustrate starting small:

- *In a metropolitan suburb, many organizations served the same families. Knowing that a shared intake form would benefit the families and save time and money, the organizations collaborated to develop a single intake form. Successfully completing this project, the members discovered they had formed a strong bond that allowed them to consider even larger joint projects.*

> "
> *Three brick layers were asked what they were doing. One said, 'I'm laying bricks.' The second replied, 'I'm building a wall.' The third stated, 'I'm constructing a temple.'*
>
> *—Anonymous*
> "

- *An urban collaboration hoped to create a city-wide model for providing respite services. Instead, the members discovered neighborhoods in which small pilot projects could prove the usefulness of their model. They focused first on building small local collaborations, and later on creating a city-wide collaboration based on the success of these smaller projects.*

In the first example, the collaboration started small and learned it could do more. In the second example, the group knew its mission would take years to achieve, so it started small with pilot projects in the hope of growing later. In both cases, the collaborations needed success in a reasonable time.

Don't Raise a Star Child

Where a pilot project is needed, avoid devoting so much time and effort to it that the "regular" workers and projects are neglected. This fosters bad feelings at the mildest, and official rebukes for favoritism at the worst. Keep a careful balance in mind so that the collaboration pilot gets the resources and support it needs without swallowing up all the resources and support other emerging projects need.

To develop an action plan, review with the whole group what the collaborative action is likely to achieve. Develop a strategy to make the best use of existing resources and powers. Then decide whether or not to begin with a pilot project.

Choosing a Pilot Project

When choosing a pilot project, consider these questions:

- Does the pilot showcase the potential of the collaborative vision?

- What small-scale action could help convince funders, power brokers, and the larger community to support the collaboration?

- Does the pilot take into account the needs of the consumer? (Select a project that reflects real client or community needs. While the pilot may not address all areas of concern, it can persuade people to support the collaboration by showing them that the community benefits.)

- Can the pilot be evaluated in a timely manner?

- How soon must the collaboration show results? (Because many collaborations take years to mature and show large-scale results, consider choosing a pilot that favors speed over output.)

- Who is the audience for the pilot program? (The collaboration may need to prove itself to an agency executive or a group of legislators long before it provides evidence to the community. Or, the collaboration may need to prove the benefits of collaboration to peers and co-workers before approaching more powerful groups.)

- Does the pilot help the collaboration mature? (The pilot must interest most members of the collaboration. Avoid building great strength in one program area because this limits the collaboration's ability to adapt.)

Create Accountability Standards

Accountability is proof of action. To be accountable, we create standards by asking questions such as: "How will we know if our associates are living up to their side of the deal?" "How will each of us know if we've done enough, or need to do more?" (We can later use these accountability standards to evaluate our work.) Let's look at several accountability descriptions:

- *Mary is responsible for all communications. She writes all memos and letters, and responds to all written communications.*

- *The executive director of each member organization will ensure full communication of all information about the collaboration directly to respective boards. Notice of such communications will be sent to the collaboration secretary for our records.*

- *The XYZ agency is the fiscal agent for this collaboration and is accountable for all areas of financial management, including but not limited to:*
    - *Receiving grant moneys and other funds.*
    - *Dispersing funds according to collaboration agreements.*
    - *Maintaining records of all transactions.*
    - *Reporting to the collaboration and funding sources as required.*

To prepare these descriptions, brainstorm possible accountability standards, refine them using a subgroup, and review them with the total group. Then include them in the action plan.

Build Collaborative Work Habits

Output and action through collaboration require new work skills. Those of us who work our way through Stages 1 and 2 come to think about work in a different way. As one partner said, "Now, I have to think of everybody all the time, not just the fastest way to get the job done. It's like marrying into a family with lots of kids; suddenly it's not just me anymore."

Be aware that those people who have not participated intimately in the development of the collaboration will likely need training and coaching in order to work collaboratively. For everyone involved, build the following collaborative work habits:

> "
> *We never know, believe me, when we have succeeded best.*
>
> — *Miguel de Unamuno (1864–1936) Spanish philosopher*
> "

> *You don't manage people; you manage things. You lead people.*
>
> — *Grace Hooper American admiral*

For Leaders and Decision Makers

- Gain commitment to strategic decisions; people support what they help create.

- Think through the impact of a decision on all those affected, not just one organization.

- Tell all the right people about all the important decisions and conversations; route important documents to them frequently.

- Share the credit for successes with everyone involved.

- Talk enthusiastically about collaboration to disperse the values of working together.

- Maintain a constant mind-set for negotiation and cooperation.

For Staff of Home Base Organizations

- Avoid adversarial language that heightens a sense of competition between home base organizations in the collaboration.

- Listen for what clients and consumers need or want to hear about the collaboration.

- Think about who else needs information.

- Ask for guidelines about specific steps the collaboration members have agreed to undertake together.

- Accept changes.

For Community Members

- Think in terms of what is best for the overall community, not just one area.

- Avoid language of right and wrong—not a "better way," but "another way."

- Think about who else needs to be involved.

- Learn to forgive.

Retreat

Because planning can be complicated, consider a retreat to plan the action, address conflicts, and emphasize the special nature of the effort. Retreats build relationships that help bridge differences and cement partnerships. Consider an outside facilitator who can focus the process and who has no stake in the actions to be taken. She or he can often help the group accomplish more, faster.

If a retreat is not possible, set a series of consecutive work sessions. Stress the importance of attending. Agree that whoever shows up will make the decisions. Above all, keep the initiative rolling.

Also pay attention to turf issues. While these can arise at any time, they are especially prone to surface now because our collaboration is making decisions about work and money, and we are involving others in the community. As partners, we must encourage each other to be open about self-interests. This is a perfect time to revisit our self-interests and invite the disclosure of others' self-interests.

Ask people within and outside the collaboration to review the plan. Try not to lose objectivity about what will and won't work. Ensure that appropriate leaders within the member organizations have reviewed the action plan and have committed—in writing—to the time and dollars necessary to make the effort happen.

Remember, collaboration is a cloverleaf that returns on itself, ever expanding and improving. We will always be revising our vision, action plans, accountabilities, and collective work habits.

The first milestone for ensuring success by working organization-to-organization is an action plan. Refer to the Action Implementation Plan in Appendix C (page 161) for a planning format and guide.

In meeting the challenge of managing the work, the milestone demonstrates our learning that output and action underlie:

- A review of the vision and desired results to confirm our destination and ensure that end users are included.

- Laying out an action plan that is specific, sets responsibilities, includes a budget, and is communicated to all appropriate people.

- Creating accountability standards so we know what we have accomplished individually and together.

- Building collaborative work habits for leaders, staff of home base organizations, and community members.

This fertile plain feels good, doesn't it? We're beginning to enjoy the benefits of all our hard work in the beginning stages of collaboration. What can be better than this? Creating joint systems.

Action Implementation Plan

> 66
>
> *Listening, not imitation, may be the sincerest form of flattery.*
>
> — *Dr. Joyce Brothers*
> *American psychologist*
>
> 99

Create Joint Systems (Challenge 3B)

Create Joint Systems

As we learn to work organization-to-organization, the emphasis changes from "What can you and I do?" to "What can our agencies do together?" Linking leaders at the collaboration table and through communication is a beginning. But now we go beyond the representatives at the table by creating interagency work groups that plan, implement, and evaluate the activities of the collaboration. We also create common forms, information systems, and operating procedures. This expands ownership and commitment.

The Tri-County group needed harmonious policies and common intake procedures, so they brainstormed the daily snafus and bigger system-wide problems the staff were encountering. This provided a list of implementation issues to improve through training or better communications, and policy issues to address on each organization's board or governing body. The steering committee enlisted representatives from various boards to draft joint policies.

Our collaboration may not need to create joint systems and policies among its member organizations. Yet joint systems and policies can help ensure our actions and output. Therefore, we will likely need to:

> **Decide the Degree of Closeness**
>
> **Create and Approve Joint Agreements**
>
> **Make Needed Organizational Changes**

Decide the Degree of Closeness

To begin, invite the whole group to decide how close the member organizations need to operate to support the collaborative structure and action plan. Here are four possible ways of coordinating the work:

- **Interagency committee:** Representatives from the member organizations participate on various committees or task forces to implement programs or services. Leadership is on a committee-by-committee basis, informal, and shared by all organizations.

- **Single point:** A key organization coordinates program activities or services as agreed with the other organizations. Leadership, which rests with the single organization, is fairly informal.

- **Lead agency:** All member organizations sign a written agreement giving one organization greater authority and responsibility to ensure that activities or services are completed, evaluated, and supported.

- **Incorporation:** In planning how to structure the work, some collaborations discuss incorporation in which representatives of the collaborative members become the board of the new corporation. A corporation, however, takes on a life of its own and soon begins to define the vision, relationships, and action steps in terms that may no longer serve the member organizations. According to the definition used in this book, the corporation is then no longer a collaboration, because the corporation is no longer "mutually beneficial."

These options represent a continuum of leadership. Since all the options are valid, the key is to choose the one that gives sufficient control to move ahead, yet is not so cumbersome that we spend a lot of effort creating joint systems rather than executing our plans.

Data Privacy Issues

Data privacy acts are special challenges to collaborations. These acts were intended to protect individuals and families by prohibiting release of private information. Talk to the county district attorney or state attorney about the intent of the data privacy acts in your community and the way the local courts interpret state and federal statutes. To resolve data privacy issues, ask clients to sign a release that identifies the specific member organization in a collaboration to whom information may be released.

Create and Approve Joint Agreements

All members of the collaboration must seek approval from their home organization's leadership for the potential agreements. After initial approval is received, write interagency agreements that clarify power, authority, responsibility, and resources. A legal document may not be necessary, but some form of written communication is needed to formalize relationships. Do this well, because clarity increases the likelihood that the organization will commit. A subgroup can draft the agreements to present to the total group.

Next, each home base organization needs to ask:

- What policies, procedures, and operations must we institute to support the work of the collaboration?

- What policies, procedures, and operations do we need to change or eliminate because they obstruct cooperation?

We're still not where we're going but we're still not where we were.

*— Natasha Josefowitz
French-American
writer and lecturer*

"

The more laws and order are made prominent, the more thieves and robbers there will be.

— Lao Tsu (c. 604–c. 531 B.C.E.) Chinese philosopher

"

Each member organization asks these questions to ensure that the collaboration's proposed activities won't compromise that organization's mission, values, resources, or image; and to be sure that the work of the collaboration will strengthen each organization.

Of course, what our collaboration needs may be in opposition to some of the operating principles of member organizations; we need to find a balance. For example, an organization's authority to spend money may be limited by board authorization, but our collaboration cannot wait for quarterly board meetings to approve funds. Some organizations have policies that hamper sharing client information such as confidential mailing lists. Here are some other examples of both restrictive and supportive policies.

Restrictive Policies:

- Limits on the hours the staff can spend working with other agencies
- Limits on the resources dedicated to interagency activities
- Strict protocols on the use of logos and focus statements
- Policies withholding client information solely to protect market share

Supportive Policies:

- Expectations about outcomes from collaboration
- Dollar expenditure limits for collaborative work, above which board approval is necessary
- Discretion for use of logos to people engaged in collaboration
- Policies that make client welfare the primary principle, regardless of who helps the client

The Nonlegal Approach

To accomplish their plans, many collaborations believe that they have to create some form of legal entity separate from the home base organizations. Not necessarily so! One organization may take fiscal responsibility; another might manage communications; yet another might coordinate providing the services or products. Written agreements are important, but beware of spending too much time on creating legally binding joint systems, which might be just another excuse for avoiding conflict, not taking action, or skirting accountability. Get started. Form legal entities later, if necessary, after achieving some results.

A Training Opportunity

Reviewing policies that may restrict collaboration can be a great opportunity for training board and team members in the art of collaboration and policy making. Many organizations labor under boards that manage tiny details instead of the big picture. Discussions about whether a certain policy is restrictive can spread values and ideas about how to make and nurture good policies, as well as good collaboration. Involving high-level and powerful people in the effort is important because they can speed the development and passage of important policies and regulations that support collaboration. An outside facilitator might be helpful. She or he can often help focus the process.

The collaboration and the home base organizations need to negotiate joint agreement on policies, procedures, and operations. To reach agreement, select two or three representatives from the collaboration to work with all the organizations. Finalize the joint agreement with a single document containing all the appropriate signatures. Remember, the higher the level of signature, the better for long-term support.

Make Needed Organizational Changes

To support the collaborative effort, member organizations may need to change some of their operating policies and procedures. This often requires the involvement of board or senior officials. Policies guide expectations; expectations guide the way in which work is done. Only through policy level changes can we permanently alter the way in which work gets done.

This is one of the places where tracking all the milestones pays off. The completed worksheets (or whatever form of documentation the collaboration has chosen) can be reviewed by all concerned in each home base organization. A great deal of education of the entire organization is necessary, an effort which should have been ongoing. In any case, complete records on the collaboration's vision, desired results, structure, action plan, and so on, will help member organizations make the internal changes they need to support the work of collaboration.

Each member of our collaboration follows up with her or his organization to ensure that needed policies, procedures, and operations are in writing and have been instituted. Then we record these changes because they are important for both evaluation and historical documentation.

The formal agreements are also perfect products for public relations, media attention, and convincing others that our collaboration is working.

◆ ◆ ◆

Joint agreements are the milestone for the challenge of creating joint systems. Refer to Joint Agreements in Appendix C (page 163) for a checklist of items to be covered.

In erecting this milestone, we realize that output and action are the foundation for:

Joint Agreements

• Deciding on a degree of closeness between organizations that gives both sufficient control to move ahead yet is not cumbersome.

- Creating and approving joint agreements on policies, procedures, and operations.

- Making needed organizational changes so that internal policies and procedures support the collaboration.

Let's take a moment to look at what's happening on the fertile plains. All of our planning is paying off. Together, we have created a record of our joint efforts. Our next challenge: evaluating the work we've done.

Evaluate the Results

Evaluate the Results (Challenge 3C)

At the thought of evaluation, the gut tightens, the stomach churns. We feel judged; our self-esteem is at stake. Even if our reaction is milder, we often see evaluation as drudgery and paperwork.

Evaluation loomed over the Tri-County collaboration. No one knew just how to approach it. The steering committee asked members to attend a bimonthly meeting prepared to evaluate the pilot projects. At the meeting, everyone realized that the results were not uniform, so the group began to use client surveys, funder questionnaires, and financial reviews to measure success. Results really showed up when the partners shared this information. Then they discovered how far they had come on the journey.

Evaluation is a discovery, and it should be a positive experience. Through evaluation we learn how successful we are at achieving our destination— our community benefits and separate self-interests. We also learn what works and what doesn't. To evaluate the work, our collaboration must:

> **Value Evaluation**
>
> **Create an Evaluation Plan**
>
> **Continually Improve the Work**

Value Evaluation

We need to tailor evaluation to our unique collaboration. To do this, discuss what evaluation can teach the collaboration, what potential effects it will have on the joint effort and on the stakeholders, and what others in similar efforts can learn from our successes and failures. Here are some approaches that help the collaboration value evaluation:

- **View evaluation as reflection.** Avoid assuming that the actions we chose are the best or the only ways to achieve results. Healthy collaborations evolve; they are open to modification and improvement.

- **Integrate evaluation into the work.** Evaluation needs to be integral to our collaborative effort, not imposed from the outside. Those of us who created the collaboration must involve ourselves in the decision about how to design and implement the evaluation.

- **Tailor evaluation to the stage of collaboration.** The results of new collaborations differ from those of well-established efforts. In the beginning, our collaboration's only data may be the process milestones we've accomplished. Later we may be able to provide information on whether we are achieving results.

- **Use multiple methods.** Evaluation needs to capture diverse patterns through both qualitative and quantitative methods.

- **Evaluate results and processes.** The milestone worksheets help document and evaluate our processes, while we can measure our results against the concrete measures we established when we first began our collaboration.

- **Appreciate failure.** Be up-front about aborted efforts or fiascoes. These needn't defeat us. In fact, they can strengthen us. Acknowledging a flop is especially important when key decision makers, such as government officials and funders, are involved. Interest them in problem solving, fully inform them of mistakes, and invite them to see the failure as a learning opportunity.

- **Expect rich information.** The same actions can influence recipients of the collaborative effort in many different ways. Moreover, many different actions can influence a given recipient toward a given result. Thus, we must acknowledge the reality of both multiple results from a given effort and multiple variables influencing a given result.

> *True science teaches, above all, to doubt and be ignorant.*
>
> — *Miguel Unamuno (1864–1936) Spanish philosopher*

Prove It!

Often we hope that an evaluation will "prove" that our work resulted in specific outcomes. Because collaborations try to achieve major changes with multiple results and variables, such proof is rare if not impossible to come by. But we can sometimes find correlations between our actions and changes in the community. While not proof of our success, such correlations support our case. They help us show the community that the collaboration was effective.

To know that you do not know is the best. To pretend to know when you do not know is a disease.

— *Lao Tsu (c. 604–c. 531 B.C.E.) Chinese philosopher*

Create an Evaluation Plan

After beginning to value evaluation, we proceed to set up measures and methods. While evaluation ideally needs to begin from the first meeting, most collaborations do not formalize assessment until they are ready to act. Yet we need to continually measure performance against expectations in both process—how the group functions, and results—what the group achieves.

Process Evaluation

1. State the separate self-interests of each organization and how it will know its self-interests are being met.

2. Note when milestones are accomplished and what helped and hindered their accomplishment.

3. Describe communication processes between members of the collaboration.

4. Summarize the collaboration's impact on its member organizations. What has each contributed? How did the collaboration change the way each organization does business?

5. Note side effects. Who else became involved because of the collaboration? How does their involvement help the cause?

Results Evaluation

1. State the desired community benefits (for example, reduction in homelessness) and how the collaboration will know if the effort is successful.

2. Outline the methods being used, such as lobbying, delivery of services, creation of information packets.

3. Summarize critical junctures. (For example, while a collaboration may be unable to prove that it reduced homelessness, it can note an important accomplishment, such as a drive to change zoning ordinances that resulted in increased permits for low-cost housing.)

4. Describe how the characteristics of the community being targeted (geographic, ethnic population, sector, field, service recipient) have changed, the number and diversity of the people involved, their reaction to the collaboration and its methods, and changes in the community that might be attributed to the effort.

5. Note side effects. (For example, the city council voted to rezone and is now more involved in the issues of homelessness. The neighborhood, however, protests low income housing.)

If our collaboration has observed its milestones, we now have data we need. If not, we go back and review the previous steps and ensure that we have completed and gathered all the documents. Next, ask a subgroup to lay out the data so that it fits into the various process and results categories. At this time, the subgroup creates other categories as needed, then assigns responsibilities for seeking other data (if needed), analyzing information, and summarizing findings. If all this seems formidable, contact someone who specializes in evaluation.

Finally, the whole group reviews the plan. Then we ask key decision makers in our home base organizations and other important stakeholders if the plan will provide the information they need to continue supporting our collaborative effort. After making any needed changes, we ratify the evaluation plan.

Continually Improve the Work

Collaborations must constantly seek feedback by listening everywhere, and continually assess their efforts in accord with their developmental stage. The purpose is continuous improvement. Thus, evaluation becomes integral to the joint effort. What questions do we ask on an ongoing basis?

- **Is the effort effective?** Are we achieving our objectives by benefiting the community and meeting our own self-interests?

- **Is the effort adequate?** Are we using enough resources to achieve results?

- **Is the effort efficient?** Have we expended minimum time, money, and energy to build maximum relationships and take complete action?

- **What lessons have we learned?** What do we now know about the relationships we have built and need to build, and the work we have done and need to do?

Honest answers to these questions create opportunities for further change, refinements, and improved results. Communicating those results builds increased support from member organizations and from those who might be persuaded to join the effort.

> "
> *and if ever i touched a life i hope that life knows that i know that touching is and always will be the true revolution.*
>
> — *Nikki Giovanni American author*
> "

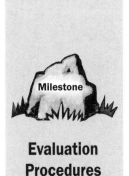

Evaluation Procedures

The milestone at this point in the journey is the evaluation plan. Refer to Evaluation Procedures in Appendix C (page 165) for a review of what to include in creating an evaluation plan.

In placing this milestone by the road, we have learned how output and action underlie our ability to:

- Value evaluation and tailor the evaluation to our unique collaboration.

- Create an evaluation plan that continually measures performance against expectations in both process—how the group functions, and results—what the group achieves.

- Continually improve our work by seeking feedback everywhere and learning from the information.

As travelers we are proud of our progress and accomplishments. What next? We must begin to renew the effort!

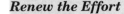

Renew the Effort

Renew the Effort (Challenge 3D)

Remember, the sole purpose of collaboration is for organizations to achieve results they are more likely to achieve together than alone. Sometimes the purpose of the group becomes fixed, and it disregards evaluative data that demands a change in practice. To achieve both our self-interests and community benefits, we must accept the validity of evaluation information, especially when it says that we—individually and organizationally—are part of the problem.

To address the problems and renew our effort, we must:

Promote Adaptability and Flexibility

Retire Appropriate Members

Add New Members

Celebrate, Celebrate

Promote Adaptability and Flexibility

To avoid the rigidity that can set in, we must work at being adaptable and flexible. Adaptability is the capacity to adjust to major changes in the community we serve; that is, we adapt to changing external forces. Flexibility is the capacity of our collaboration to remain open to varied ways of organizing itself. We need to see ourselves as temporary and constantly evolving.

Our collaboration uses information from evaluation and other sources to renew its output and action. A review of the previous eleven challenges can help us change either the objectives or the process of collaboration.

The Tri-County partners experienced many positive results, but the work overwhelmed them. Some felt that collaboration was becoming an unpaid, part-time job. In response, each shelter identified one staff person to work full time providing care and coordinating programs. Moreover, two new organizations paid for part-time positions to support the collaboration. After one team issued a report that documented change, the steering group threw a holiday party to celebrate the enormous success of the program.

Just as the Tri-County group was adaptable and flexible, we need to discuss the evaluation to date and what is working and what is not. Use the following questions:

- What is changing among member organizations, in the community, and in social, political, and economic trends?

- What is changing in our collaboration itself?

- What must we change to be more adaptable and flexible?

- Who has finished their work for the collaboration?

- How should we ask them to leave?

- Who else needs to be involved to further the effort? In other words, what powers and preferences do we need now?

- How should we approach new members?

- How should we orient them?

- What is the best structure for the re-formed collaboration?

- How will we celebrate what we have accomplished and the people who have helped us accomplish these things?

Consider taking time for a special "renewal meeting." This can be critical for collaboration. All too often we bemoan our failures and simply move on or move into trying to fix problems. What we need to do instead is to study both our failures *and* successes, review the membership (our relationships) and the challenges (the work we have to do), and use this information to renew the effort.

> "
> *Pay attention to the questions you need to ask, not the answers you want to hear.*
>
> *— Leonard Hirsch*
> *American consultant*
> "

Retire Appropriate Members

Retiring or "sunsetting" people and organizations is not easy, but at this point in our journey, we probably have less need for people who envision and empower than for those who ensure success through attention to details, procedures, and implementation. The following story illustrates the need to retire members:

> *A group of eleven educational institutions and organizations were collaborating on training, purchasing, and other specific administrative functions. Two members were cautious and refused to move ahead; they worried that the State Department of Education was not satisfied with the work the collaboration was doing. Others members were pleased with the progress. Eventually, the members agreed to disagree so that these two people and their organizations could leave graciously.*

A discussion of what our collaborative group needs and who can best meet those needs will likely manage the issue of sunsetting. The convener raises the question; as a group, we provide the answers and reward our partners as they leave.

Do not use sunsetting to avoid conflict. But if all other avenues have failed and the member does not see that his or her contribution is hindering the relationships and work, ask the person to leave. Remember, the collaboration originally asked this person (and organization) to join because he or she had something to contribute. So if sunsetting is the best decision, be considerate and careful; don't burn bridges. Here are some points to consider when sunsetting a member:

- The member's home base organization may need more education about the effort and how the collaboration can meet both community needs and the self-interests of its members. This might allow the organization to educate its representative or send a better-qualified person.

Keeping Leaders Committed

After the actual work has begun, many of the more powerful collaborative leaders lose interest. That's because high-level administrators, board members, or officials are often more interested in broad policy than day-to-day work. Yet if their leadership drifts away, our collaboration may drift too. To keep these leaders committed, involve them in deciding how the changes actually benefit the community and how the changes can be institutionalized. (This tendency for leaders to drift at this stage of group development underscores the importance of having *both* policy makers and implementers involved from the beginning.)

- Another person from the same home base organization may be a more amenable or capable representative. This may also allow the organization to save face by stating that the person leaving is needed elsewhere.

- A power broker in the home base organization may be blocking the efforts of the representative. All members need to help the organization deal with this issue in the context of the collaboration. (See Think Strategically, page 67.)

- The person or home base organization may be much more useful later in the collaboration's life. Ask the organization's leaders to postpone its involvement. Promise to keep them fully informed.

Add New Members

In response to our collaboration's changing needs, we may seek new members. While we may have been bringing in new people all along, formal or informal evaluation tells us what powers to add and what style preferences to search for. At this stage in the collaboration, we'll most likely need:

- Task-oriented players who might have found the first two stages too slow.

- Staff who are likely to implement the changes.

- Consumers or end users who will benefit from the collaboration's efforts. (If earlier planning was frustrating for them, this time for action can be exciting.)

First, we establish guidelines for adding members and develop more formal orientation plans. Then, as we add new members, we need to help them learn our culture. To do this, revisit the trust-building steps followed during the early stages of collaboration. Insert all documents in a folder to be given to the new member. Assign a "buddy" who will review the vision, desired results, structure, and evaluation plans with the new member. Ask what the new member needs in terms of self-interests, customs, languages, and preferences. Confirm what powers the member can contribute (see pages 29–33 to review). After everyone has had time to build relationships, assign responsibilities to the new member.

As a group, review the structure, because the addition of new members might require changes. (For example, a group may change from the table model to the wheel model, especially if the group is beginning to exceed fifteen people.) Also reexamine the action plan and the joint agreements. Modify them as needed to accommodate the new members and new home base organizations.

> **"**
>
> *Evaluation is by feedback, not by autopsy.*
>
> *— Karen Ray*
> *American consultant and author*
>
> **"**

Celebrate, Celebrate

Everyone in our collaboration and all our supporters need to feel involved, useful, and valued. As a group, reward those staying and those leaving for their efforts. At this point, the greatest reward is public recognition.

One collaboration on family violence held an all-day conference and celebration after months of work. Each action team presented its key discoveries in video, drama, or music format — no traditional speeches. Data were available in a beautifully assembled summary booklet. A band played; a singer conveyed many of the emotions of those involved in the issues of abuse. Four hundred people celebrated, joined arm in arm, laughed, cried. And then the work continued, renewed, with new people involved.

This celebration was a big "bash." But our celebration need not be large. What's important? Recognizing established members of the collaboration and creating an opportunity to include new people who might renew the work.

◆ ◆ ◆

The last milestone for ensuring success by working organization-to-organization is documented changes. Refer to Checklist for Changes in Appendix C (page 167) for a further review.

In meeting the last challenge of Stage 3—renew the effort—we have learned that output and action are the foundation for:

- Promoting adaptability and flexibility to adjust to changes in the community and to remain open to varied ways of organizing ourselves.

- Retiring appropriate members so the collaboration has the skills and powers to continue its work.

- Adding new members and orienting them to the collaboration.

- Remembering to celebrate accomplishments and reward both those who are staying and those who are leaving.

In Stage 3, we got to enjoy the benefits of our hard labor. Together we built the organization-to-organization relationships that ensure success. Now we move to Stage 4, of creating, sustaining, and enjoying collaboration. ◆

Milestone

Checklist for Changes

Stage 4: Endow Continuity by Working Collaboration-to-Community

Gathering Building Materials for the Future from the Broad Forest

I n Stage 4, our collaboration finally moves into the broad forest. In Stage 3, we worked organization-to-organization, and we were very productive. We thought we had arrived at our destination and could rest there—and for some collaborations, that is indeed the case. But others of us see the broad forest on the horizon and wonder what resources exist there that might fulfill our potential. So we travel again, arriving at the edge of the forest, gathering building materials for the future by working collaboration-to-community to endow the continuity of our results.

We accomplish continuity when our collaboration increases relationships and responsibilities in the greater community. Let's be clear here: continuity means the continuance of the *collaborative effort,* not the *collaboration group.* Even as we prepare to leave or end the collaboration, we want the community to accept what we have started and to nurture it as part of larger community efforts. Two anecdotes reveal the desire groups have for the larger community to both embrace the results of the collaborative work and increase its impact:

- *A youth-serving organization that is creating a community-wide, workforce-development strategy wants to see its effort go beyond demonstration projects. It wants the strategy to be integral to every school's curriculum, supported by government jobs and training, and augmented by all post-secondary institutions—academic and vocational.*

> "
> *The future of mankind lies waiting for those who come to understand their lives and take up their responsibilities to all living things.*
>
> — *Vine Victor Deloria, Jr. Standing Rock Sioux author*
> "

- *One city's African American community has made progress in articulating values and starting a foundation to foster economic development. But to make a strong impact, many more people will need to embrace and acclaim its values. Many funders will have to endow the foundation so it can spur African American economic development throughout the city.*

For collaborative efforts to succeed over time, many people need to understand the magnitude and implications of the work we do. Our collaboration's story has to spread to endow the effort with support. We spread word of our success through myths—stories we tell others about our results.

The word myth is commonly used to connote something not true. But myths are actually stories explaining phenomena, such as war, love, puberty, and aging. Through language and symbol, myths shape people's interpretation of events and introduce new ways of understanding what has been achieved. The following story illustrates the birth of a myth:

> *A collaboration between the state and local school districts channeled grants directly to classroom teachers to fund experimental curricula. The steering committee for the collaboration met regularly in different sites throughout the state. To reach the meeting site, members of the committee car-pooled, chatting freely on the drive. The story grew that this group knew everybody in the state who was doing exciting new work. The myth was created that this committee kept things moving with useful information and the latest ideas.*

Collaborations convey myths in personal contact and through the media. These myths spread the word about our achievements, attract people to our effort, and give our founders status and credibility, which helps them attract and train new leaders. This is important because by involving more people and having greater impact, we build for the future.

While continuity and myth are always present, they are crucial to the last four key challenges of our journey:

Create Visibility

Involve the Community

Change the System

End the Collaboration

66

To love what you do and feel that it matters—how could anything be more fun.

— *Katherine Graham American newspaper publisher*

99

Create Visibility (Challenge 4A)

Our collaboration needed resources early on to build relationships and to work. That's why we emphasized communications with all stakeholders. Now we need community-wide resources to endow the continuity of effort because projects that will have a strong impact on the community require broad legitimacy. Effective collaborations tell their myths before this point. But now is the time for a concerted effort.

By its second winter, the Tri-County collaboration had done its work. Stories abounded about how the collaboration could slay giants. Throughout the community, funders, executives, board members, the public in general transmitted the myth. The media covered the story—it was news! The collaboration clearly had a public relations plan that was working.

We, too, need to:

Convey an Image

Promote the Results

Create Visibility

Convey an Image*

To gain major support from the community, our collaboration must be seen as a leader. Our image is crucial. It must grab the hearts of people. And the simpler the message, the more room each heart will give it. Two anecdotes reveal the power of an image.

- *One collaboration wanted to convey the image of being purposeful and quick to bring diverse groups together. They created a video of a group of people (representing the diverse groups they wanted to be seen as reaching) sitting in a circle of swivel chairs facing out—backs to each other. In the video, the leader of the collaboration approaches everyone in turn asking them to participate. Each person declines for various reasons.*

  The leader then moves decisively and turns each chair around so all people are facing into the circle. She sits in the one empty chair, passes out papers to everyone saying that here are possible ways of working together. Everyone looks at her or his paper, and all are heard to say in their own way that there are some possibilities here. The videotape ends.

---

* *Materials on image and promotion were adapted from* Marketing Workbook for Nonprofit Organizations *by Gary Stern, available from Fieldstone Alliance.*

> "
> *All paths lead to the same goal: to convey to others what we are. And we must pass through solitude and difficulty, isolation and silence, in order to reach forth to the enchanted place...*
>
> — *Pablo Neruda (1904–1973) Nobel Prize winning Chilean author*
> "

• *Another group wanted to be seen as a leader in reducing family violence, so they developed a public demonstration to underscore the roots of abuse. In the demonstration, eight people, each holding a blanket, stand behind a woman. The woman sits in a chair. A narrator explains that this woman had suffered abuse from her husband and found it difficult to leave the situation.*

After the explanation, a man representing her father puts a blanket over the woman, saying that she must obey her father. When the woman protests, a woman representing her mother places another blanket over her, saying that "father knows best." A woman representing a teacher places a third blanket over the seated woman, admonishing her to follow the rules and sit in her chair. A fourth blanket is placed over the seated woman by a man representing her minister who tells her the Bible says she must obey her husband. This continues until all eight blankets are on her.

The narrator then says to the seated woman, "You're an adult. You're intelligent. Why don't you leave your husband? Why do you tolerate his abuse? Fight back!" The woman attempts to fight through eight blankets. She is almost paralyzed. Then, one by one, the people remove the blankets, briefly describing what each of these important figures in her life can do to help her deal with the abuse. The underlying message is that the collaboration will help make this possible.

In just a few minutes, with just a few words, both these collaborations communicated a strong image. How can we do this? First, brainstorm answers to the following questions:

• What myths can we tell about how the collaboration began and evolved, and the results we have achieved?

• What images—the combination of words, pictures, shapes, colors, and sounds—convey what we've done and who we are?

• What symbols can we use to convey those images and tell our stories?

A Stranger in a Strange Land

Going public about a collaboration is like being a stranger in a strange land. We don't know what to expect or how we'll be perceived. At first, we're leery of funders' reactions, of other colleagues' responses, of the community's ability to understand. We talk little of our problems and more about the possibility of changes.

Gradually, we reveal what's good in this new way of doing things. We acknowledge how hard the journey has been. We begin to influence those around us to think about how collaboration might strengthen their accustomed ways of getting the job done. This is the way the community benefits.

Have a subgroup refine these ideas into an image statement that is more than words and sends the right message about the collaboration. Review it with others to determine its impact. Refine it as needed. Then, as a group ratify the image and convey it everywhere.

Promote the Results

With myths to relate and an image to convey, the collaboration now promotes its results. We've actually been promoting our achievements all along. Every time we communicate the vision, describe the collaboration process, state our actions, and so on, we are promoting results. To be really effective, we need to realize that all along we must relate what we are doing and act to build the relationships we need, because we—individually and collectively—are a role model for the community.

But now, we approach promotion more deliberately. We develop and implement a promotion plan that will include many more people and resources to endow our effort and increase our impact over time. So we approach promotion by answering the following questions:

- **Do we have a promotional message that motivates our audience to take action?**
  The overall message needs to be consistent, but we are seeking different responses from specific audiences. So we need to tailor some of our message to particular publics. No matter who we are addressing, the message needs to be in the everyday language of that audience. We already know what our publics want (see Think Strategically, page 67); now we must be clear about the response we want—enrollments, purchases, referrals, donations, volunteer time.

- **What specific next steps are we asking our publics to take?**
  For example, to ask people to donate may be a big leap. To ask them to make a no-obligation phone call to learn more about the benefits to the community and potential donors is less of a request (and more likely to get a response). The message conveys the specific step, not the overall program. Above all, the benefit to the public must be clear.

- **How will we promote the message?**
  We need to consider a variety of techniques: advertising, billboards, annual reports, brochures, celebrity endorsements, direct mail, editorials, feature stories, letters to the editors, networking, news conferences, news releases, newsletters, posters, public speaking, public service announcements, publishing articles and reports, special events, talk shows, trade fairs, videos, word of mouth.

> *Political communication is intended to move people, not relate information.*
>
> — Leonard Hirsch
> American consultant

" *Communication is a marketable asset.*

— *Susan Sampsell American businesswoman*

"

" *Perserverance and audacity generally win.*

— *Dorothee DeLuzy (1747–1830) French actress*

"

Regardless of the technique, gear the approach to the particular public; plan how each technique can be used to maximum effect; use a mix of techniques; repeat the message frequently over an extended period of time; experiment and when the experiment works, do it again; don't be seduced by glamour; and persevere.

Here are some specific techniques that have been used successfully:

- Stories from clients and consumers about how things have improved

- A breakfast for funders to "tell the truth about how we got here"

- Data summaries from the evaluation sent to every legislator

- Data summaries from the evaluation sent periodically to every foundation that has some interest in the collaboration's effort

- An article published in the local United Way's newsletter about the collaboration

- A one-page description of the collaboration and its values included in every employee handbook in every participating organization

- Local news coverage of the benefits and cost-effectiveness of collaboration, using a message that's simple and compelling

- Luncheons, dinners, and socials to thank staff and supporters for implementing the work

- Thank-you letters to key people involved at every stage, proclaiming the successes and thanking them for their contribution

- Thank-you letters to the associates, superiors, employees, and families of people involved, thanking them for supporting the collaboration member.

Have a subcommittee flesh out the responses to the questions on page 121 and the suggestions above. This committee then details the necessary steps of who will do what, by when, and with what resources. The collaboration reviews and approves the promotion plan.

Now we go to work. We turn loose those who like to tell stories; take community leaders to lunch; hold public meetings; involve the media; tell the story over and over again; relate how the collaboration's work benefits the community; tell everyone what's been learned; and declare the potential for continuing the effort.

One common thread pervades community change theories: communities are improved because individuals convince other individuals to think and act differently. Some people do feel coerced; others are enthusiastic. No matter the response, we give one gift: our results.

◆ ◆ ◆

The first milestone in Stage 4 of endowing continuity by working collaboration-to-community is a promotional plan. The resources are out there. Accomplishing the milestone taps these resources. Refer to Promotional Plan in Appendix C (page 169) for a guide to creating visibility.

In meeting the challenge of creating visibility, the milestone demonstrates our learning that continuity and myth underlie:

- Conveying an image—a combination of words, pictures, colors, and sounds—to relate what we have accomplished and who we are.

- Creating a plan to promote our results.

We have braved our way into the broad forest. We send messengers back to the people on the fertile plain: "This forest is rich! It offers even more resources than the plains, and the opportunity for greater impact." Now we face another challenge: integrating the benefits of collaboration into the community.

Promotional Plan

Involve the Community (Challenge 4B)

Our collaboration began when we realized we could achieve better results together than alone. Creating visibility was our way of obtaining greater resources for a greater impact of *our* effort.

But now, we learn that the community will have increased benefit when a larger assembly than the one we first brought together sustains the effort and increases the resources. So we begin to involve the community, not to promote our effort but to lay the groundwork for a succession plan, a process that endows communal benefits over a much longer period of time.

Fortunately, the Tri-County partners realized that a greater endowment was needed. After almost two years of working together and achieving results, they went on a retreat. There, Marjorie called for ideas to generate new interest and attract new resources for the homeless.

Involve the Community

The members planned how to train other staff in existing shelters, how to educate the community to promote partnerships to serve shelter clients, and how to convince the legislature to reward agencies that saved money by working together. Clearly, the Tri-County collaboration was integrating the benefits of collaboration into the community.

We can do this too if we:

Teach the Value of Collaboration

Bring Diverse Interests Together

Build Leadership

Hold Public Forums

Teach the Value of Collaboration

Our collaboration has been creating visibility for itself and promoting its results. Now we have to educate the larger community about the value and potential of collaboration. This provides opportunities for people to examine their beliefs about the way work gets done to both produce communal benefit and further separate self-interests. Three brief stories illustrate how groups teach the value of collaboration:

- *A family violence collaboration dedicated a small percentage of its total budget to national training. They sought opportunities to present seminars on collaboration at national conferences. Those that heard the message realized that they, too, could begin similar efforts in their communities.*

- *A literacy group wrote a brief article outlining the advantages and disadvantages of collaboration, then placed the article in newsletters and professional publications. The response indicated that many communities in the country were eager to learn how to improve literacy through collaboration.*

- *Each member organization of a food shelf collaboration dedicated a portion of its training budget to promoting collaboration in the community. The response not only increased volunteers, it led to a forum on the need to go beyond food distribution and regain the focus on eliminating hunger.*

How to teach the value of collaboration? Ask a subcommittee to outline educational strategies. Then strategize how best to leverage resources to reach the most people. (Follow the patterns used in Think Strategically, page 67, and Promote the Results, page 121.)

> "
> *Isolation is the worst possible counselor.*
>
> — *Miguel de Unamuno (1864–1936) Spanish philosopher*
> "

Bring Diverse Interests Together

To endow continuity for our collaborative effort and thereby increase impact, we must bring diverse interests together, find common purposes, and build linkages. To make this happen:

- **Identify potential representatives of diverse community interests.** Finding common ground and shared interests with these groups is crucial. Focus especially on those groups that have not been previously involved.

- **Create an open and accessible decision-making process.** This increases ownership in the community both in terms of the number and diversity of participants.

- **Adjust programs and policies to benefit the community.** Collaborations can fail when costs outweigh benefits. When we ignore changing community needs, policies and programs quickly become outmoded or counterproductive. (See Adaptability and Flexibility, page 110.)

- **Increase the base of support.** The availability of resources determines the degree to which the collaboration's efforts become permanently integrated into the community and the size of the community that will benefit.

A subcommittee drafts recommendations on the above; the whole group discusses who will and won't be involved and the implications of these decisions. While the collaboration seeks the greatest involvement of diverse groups, not all interests are able or willing to join. (See Think Strategically, page 67.)

Next, convene a meeting of the new representatives to build trust, modify the vision, and enhance the desired results and strategies (revisit Stage 1 for details). In Stage 3, we added new members to help further the efforts of our collaboration. Now, we are adding new members who will be the future leaders of an expanded effort (remember, the collaboration as we've know it will soon come to an end). Then create opportunities to involve the new members in rethinking organizational roles, organizing the enhancement effort, doing the work, and evaluating the results (see Stages 2 and 3 for details). This process is part of the cloverleaf on our journey. Thus, while moving onward in Stage 4, we return to the earlier stages with more players involved in a larger purpose.

> **"**
> *...bring people together, set up forums and conversations, celebrate our humanity, our capacity for affection.*
>
> *— Henry Cisneros Secretary of HUD*
> **"**

> **"**
> *There are no problems—only opportunities to be creative.*
>
> *— Dorye Roettger American author and public speaker*
> **"**

Build Leadership

Our community will be improved by using what the collaboration has taught it and by developing new leadership beyond the leadership that already resides in the collaboration. At this stage, leadership for the collaboration's destination needs to move from the collaboration to the community. To move leadership into a larger community, discuss these four questions.

1. **How can member organizations increase their leadership of collaboration?** Here are ways to build *organizational* leadership for collaboration:

- Boards of Directors receive training in collaboration, adopt policies in support of collaboration, collaborate directly with other boards, and hold their executives accountable for initiating and participating in effective collaborations.

- Executives and senior staff articulate how daily work benefits from collaboration. They are specific so that people can see the real difference in the way work gets done.

- Staff receive training in specific collaboration skills, are encouraged to form and enter into collaborations, and include collaboration as a criterion in their performance reviews.

- Programs and services are developed on the basis of collaboration with other providers and the clients or consumers.

Participating organizations build leadership when they discover other places and opportunities for collaboration and help others take advantage of these opportunities.

2. **How will key stakeholders and the community at large be influenced?** Here are ways to build *collaborative* leadership:

- Elected officials and community leaders recognize differences among communities, don't impose a single structure for change across diverse communities, and invest in system change efforts over time.

- Funding bodies fund collaboration as a legitimate way of doing business that requires long-term investment and support training for collaborative leadership.

- Clients, consumers, and community members promote collaboration when it is in their best interest. Thus, they discover existing competencies and use available resources.

> 66
>
> *To produce things and rear them, to produce, but not take possession of them, to act, but not to rely on one's own ability, to lead them, but not to master them—this is called a profound and secret virtue.*
>
> — *Lao Tsu*
> *(c. 604–c. 531 B.C.E.)*
> *Chinese philosopher*
>
> 99

A collaboration must identify new people with vision and optimism to carry on its work or build from its base. These new people become the new initiators and conveners who develop relationships with diverse stakeholders.

3. **Who is going to fulfill the key roles that will continue the collaborative effort?** We make sure we know what we need and then we identify specific people to met those needs.

4. **How will new leaders take charge?** Members model collaboration for others; that is, they think and act in ways that promote collaboration. The challenge for members is to let go, to turn over the reins. The challenge for institutions and communities is to cultivate and support the leaders who will carry on the collaborative effort.

Hold Public Forums

Collaboration as a way of solving problems will not thrive if we don't help the community embrace the collaborative approach. To involve the community we need forums, that is, places and ways to build collaboration by exchanging information and identifying common values.

The purpose of such forums:

- Our institutions must encourage experimentation, because collaboration relies on experimentation.

- Communities must understand that no quick solutions to major problems exist, because collaboration takes time.

- Government agencies must move beyond mandating collaboration and into supporting it by funding for long-term results rather than one- or two-year cycles.

- Private funders must cease seeing collaboration as a new "program" that receives only one-year project money. Rather, they must see it as a new

> **"**
>
> *Invest in the human soul. Who knows, it might be a diamond in the rough.*
>
> *— Mary McLeod Bethune (1875–1955) American educator and writer*
>
> **"**

Good Communities, Good Leaders

Some communities just seem to "work." Such communities practice collaborative problem solving and consensus-based decision making. In contrast, faltering communities are marked by such negatives as contentiousness, frenetic activity, or apathy, to name a few.

Leaders in communities that work strive to create win/win solutions and use power to convene people. These leaders listen as much as they talk. Leaders in communities that don't work are threatened by citizen involvement, try to use their power to decide for others, and spend time trying to convince citizens to follow a predetermined course of action.

Adapted with permission from National Civic Review, *80:2, Spring 1991.*
Copyright 1991 National Civic League, Inc. All rights reserved.

approach to system-wide change that takes years to succeed, but eventually yields benefits far beyond the scope of a single new initiative.

- Community members must view the issues as large, the destinations as complex, the ways of getting there as varied, and the answers as rarely simple but possible to address.

Our collaboration, going now beyond showcasing its own success, begins to plan forums that invite discussion and challenge the assumptions that contribute to problems in the community. We return to our work plan, modifying it to include public forums and planning how to build greater ownership for the forums.

Toward the end of the four-stage journey we learn three truths:

- The demand for collaborations must come from those who will participate in them.

- The support for collaboration must come from our institutions and our communities.

- The results propel us to look at other ways to collaborate.

Once begun, we cannot stop.

A succession plan is the milestone for involving the community. Refer to Succession Planning in Appendix C (page 171) for a checklist of key factors to consider.

In erecting the milestone of succession planning, continuity and myth are part of our learning to:

- Teach the value of collaboration to the larger community so people will examine their beliefs about the way work gets done.

- Bring diverse interests together to build linkages that will increase the impact of our efforts.

- Build leadership beyond the collaboration to continue the work of the group.

- Hold public forums—places and ways to build collaboration and its impact by exchanging information and identifying common values.

We've learned a lot on our journey. Now we share the benefits of our experience with the community. Our next step: change the system that created the problems we set out to solve.

You don't truly know something yourself until you can take it from your own mind and put it into somebody else's.

— *Milt Hinton*
79-year-old jazz great

Succession Planning

Change the System (Challenge 4C)

In our complex and rapidly changing global society, we need to replace the myth of the rugged, independent individual with one of inter-dependence among people and organizations with different world views. The relationship of these people and organizations can be viewed as a system.

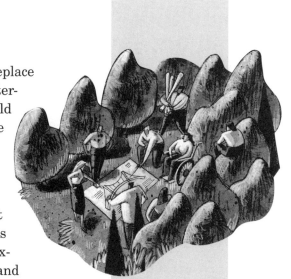

Change the System

A system is a group of key individuals and organizations that interact to produce a benefit or to maintain ways of living, working, and relating. For example, social systems exist to meet people's basic needs and manage emergencies. Justice systems preserve law and order to keep people safe. Education systems exist so people can learn, while business systems produce goods and services, offer employment, and generate revenue.

Individuals and organizations that comprise a system interact, but they are not managed. Some systems no longer provide benefits for us or don't provide them in the best ways. As a result, problems mount. When that happens, we must stop solving problems and work to change the system.

Thus, we go beyond collaboration as we know it and create a new myth. In this myth, individuals, organizations, and their separate actions merge to mobilize community-wide efforts and resources. In our new myth, when one part changes, everything changes—the system changes.

How is this new myth represented in the Tri-County story? At the retreat, Peter said, "I believe we're really talking about going beyond help for the homeless to preventing homelessness altogether." The group planned how to involve those in legislature, education, and business. When board members voiced support for the kind of system-wide changes the members wanted to work on, Betty challenged them to think about how they could develop—together—programs that would affect the whole person and the whole family. Thus, they set about changing the system that perpetuated homelessness.

To make lasting change in the community, we must:

Understand the Present System

Plan Changes in the System

Begin to Change the System

Understand the Present System

To make the substantial changes our communities need, we must push beyond the presenting problems to find their sources within the system. Service agencies and their funders and supporters help people in need; collaborations go further and achieve results that organizations are more likely to achieve together than alone. These results have impact on the larger community. But the needs of our communities are even greater yet. For lasting benefits, we need to help change the underlying system.

In our public forums, we call together many stakeholders who can:

- **Describe present conditions.** Because extensive data exists in most communities, we seldom need to gather more information.

- **Describe how people address those conditions.** To do this, we bring in the perspectives of all fields: arts, human services, environment, health care, education, media, business; and of all sectors: public, private, and nonprofit.

- **Create a clear picture of the results we want.** Let's remember that we want structural change, not more programs to alleviate problems.

Plan Changes in the System

We are raised in a culture that teaches one-thing-at-a-time linear thinking: Line up. Follow the rules. Stay within the lines. Finish one thing before beginning another. Systems thinking, however, looks at many parts of the system all at once, deals with diverse people and structures all at once, and begins multifaceted approaches to change all at once. This type of thinking uncovers the structural causes of behavior. Understanding how structure influences behavior allows everyone to see more clearly the powers to change the behavior and to adopt policies that affect the larger system.

With all the data from our forums, our collaboration proceeds to:

- **Map out all the interrelated parts of the system and how they are linked.** In relation to the desired results, we describe the impetus for and the blocks to change in each part of the system.

- **Lay out the leverage points in the system.** What are these? Those places to which we can apply pressure that will move the impetus for change forward or reduce the blocks to change. Because the exertion of leverage needs to have the greatest return for energy expended, we focus on those most likely to move. Often the leverage points are key individuals and organizations, but sometimes we must address a community-wide perspective.

> 66
>
> *Today's problems come from yesterday's solutions.*
>
> — *Peter Senge*
> *American author*
>
> 99

> 66
>
> *We are trained to seek simplicity and certainty.*
> *We must hunger for complexity and embrace ambiguity.*
>
> — *Leonard Hirsch*
> *American consultant*
>
> 99

- **Redefine the desired results from the points of view of the key stakeholders.** Language is crucial to their ability to increase the impetus for change and to reduce the blocks to change.

The collaborative approach is essential to systems thinking and systems change because no one person or organization has a full understanding of the problems, a complete picture of the desired results, or all the resources necessary to bring about major changes in complex systems.

Begin to Change the System

Systems change incorporates the basic principles of collaboration covered in the previous fourteen challenges. But in system thinking, these challenges happen on a more complex level. We have to *want* to look at that bigger picture—to develop an appetite for complexity.

What We Really Need

If collaborations are to help communities address the complexity of the problems we face, then they must focus on the underlying structure of problems, as columnist David Morris illustrates:

> People's basic need is not for electricity; it's for lighting, warmth, and mechanical power. If these things can be provided more cheaply without using electricity (by installing more windows to let in natural light, for example) or by using less electricity (by installing higher efficiency light bulbs), utilities should invest in these alternatives instead.

> Similarly, our basic need isn't for roads. We need to get to work, to shop, and to visit our friends. We can

achieve these objectives in different ways. For example, compact communities reduce the need for travel. The average household in a relatively high density central-city location drives only half as much as the average household in a low-density outer suburban location . . . . Yet urban compactness doesn't qualify for support from transportation funds.

What we *really* need are more people who are eager to work within the ambiguity and complexity inherent to any system. To foster this eagerness, our collaboration needs to embrace "systems thinking," and reward people and organizations in the community who are willing to risk this new approach.

Adapted from the work of David Morris. Used with permission.

Harnessing the Power of Systems

Think of power as two boats—one with a large engine, the other with a sail. The one with the engine consumes energy and may require more resources to operate than we have. But we need only turn the key to get it moving. While the sailboat consumes no energy, it is no good unless we know how to tap the forces that operate on

it—the system. Many people enter into collaboration believing that together they can build a bigger engine for their boats—more funds, staff, and so forth. But collaborations are really successful when they can tap the forces that drive the system.

Adapted from the work of Leonard Hirsch. Used with permission.

> In all things that are purely social we can be as separate as the fingers, yet one as the hand in all things essential to mutual progress.
>
> — *Booker T. Washington (1856–1915) American educator*

A Guide to Systems Change

To influence the system, we lay out an action plan. Our plan will:

- **Take action at the smallest level.** Individuals and small groups are easier to influence than government or multinational corporations. We can change the system "from the bottom up" by influencing the decisions and behaviors of these smaller groups. Their combined changes will alter the larger system.

- **Use multifaceted approaches in all applicable fields and sectors.** Act at many levels and in many sectors. Influence these levels simultaneously or sequentially, depending on what makes sense strategically and considering the resources available.

- **Help parts of the system form new relationships with other parts of the system.** Make connections with other systems where there have been no earlier relationships.

- **Stop and learn.** Discover what has been learned and apply this knowledge to other similar situations which in turn produce new information for others to use.

We are learning more and more about collaboration—what works and what does not. But injecting the principles of collaboration into systems change is new. Here, our collaboration moves past its initial boundaries. That is, beyond desired results to the systems level. Pushing ourselves beyond the familiar, we hunger for complexity.

◆ ◆ ◆

Uncovering the leverage points where we can begin to influence change is our milestone. Refer to A Guide to Systems Change in Appendix C (page 173) for a summary of points on beginning systems change.

When we place the milestone by the side of the road in meeting the challenge of changing the system, we have learned that continuity and myth underlie our learning to:

- Understand the present system's conditions, the sources of those conditions and a clear picture of the results we want.

- Plan changes in the system by mapping out the interrelated parts, the leverage points, and the viewpoints of key stakeholders.

- Begin to change the system.

The forest is a powerful source for new materials. We have journeyed far and come to find that as we have changed, our community has been enriched. All that remains is to look at the end of our collaboration.

End the Collaboration (Challenge 4D)

In collaboration, we keep coming back to the beginning, each time building on and improving what we've been doing. In the first three challenges of Stage 4, we move the work of the collaboration into the community. Thus, we endow our effort with support and resources, the building materials for continuity.

Turning ownership of the collaboration over to the community means that our group, as we once knew it, is coming to an end. The collaboration may not formally cease, but with so many new members, we no longer look the same. Or we may truly come to an end and bequeath our efforts to other groups and individuals who will now take the leadership.

What was this intersection like for the Tri-County partners? They held a retreat, and the members stood around the piano and sang! They had stayed the course; they had crossed the finish line; they were ready for the next race up the hillside! Joining together to celebrate accomplishments had become a ritual, so it was fitting to mark their transformation with a celebration.

Ritual endings help a collaboration change or cease as it is known. Rituals also allow the new people to begin again at Stage 1. To do this, we:

> **Understand the Need for an Ending**
>
> **Create Ending Rituals**

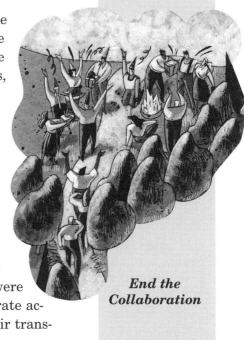

End the Collaboration

Understand the Need for an Ending

A formal ending to an existing collaborative relationship is critical for several reasons:

- **People change.** Rarely do people stay at one level in their work over long periods of time. Those who created and sustained the collaboration through its four stages may have changed. If they are to continue to value the collaboration, we need to reward them through a ritual.

- **Relationships change.** If the collaboration has been successful, there may be another around the corner. Some of the same people may be involved (especially in rural areas where there are fewer organizations and smaller populations), but because the context will be different, the relationships will change. The most powerful person in this collaboration may be only a minor player in another group, or the small player may become very important in a new situation. Ending rituals help people prepare themselves to take on new roles in new collaborations.

> 66
>
> *People change and forget to tell each other.*
>
> — *Lillian Hellman American playwright and author*
>
> 99

- **Organizations may not change.** The role the home base organizations have played may have changed only a little in comparison to the collaboration. Ending rituals free people to return fully to their organizations and their duties there.

- **Friendships are formed.** In the process of collaborating, strong bonds of friendship are often built. A ritual ending helps acknowledge that the initial basis for these friendships—collaboration—is over.

- **Endings must be marked.** For some members, the months (maybe years!) that they have dedicated to the collaboration can feel overwhelming. Ritual helps people mark the end of working together and proceed to other activities.

To prepare for a formal ending, the collaboration needs to answer the following questions:

- What do members need to feel recognized?

- What do members need to know has been accomplished?

- What has to be conveyed to the larger community to continue the effort?

- How can the ending ritual help us convey this?

- How will future work be substantially different from the way we've been doing things?

- How will we capture the history of our work together?

Create Ending Rituals

We need to celebrate the end of our collaboration—as it's been known. The celebration marks closure to a series of unique relationships and ways of working. Let's not panic here! To ritualize an ending does not mean holding a mystic or "touchy-feely" event. Our celebration simply needs to cover the following elements:

- A time and place where most of the key players can be present

- Recollections of what each person and organization contributed to the collaboration

- Involvement of as many of the supporters of the collaboration and its members as possible

- Inclusion of some myths about "how it used to be worse" or "how it was before"

- Enjoyment!

> "
> *Celebrity was a long time in coming; it will go away. Everything goes away.*
>
> — *Carol Burnett*
> *American comedienne*
> "

Here are two ways collaborations have conducted ending rituals:

- *A literacy group went back to the retreat house where they had held their first meeting. They reviewed their written history, making comments and corrections for later publication of the document. A key figure from the state office distributed certificates as a "thank you." Members then talked about what they had learned from the collaboration and about their plans for other kinds of similar work in the future. Refreshments and friendly conversation concluded their collaboration.*

- *Another group, which had worked together for four years, always traveled some distance to attend meetings. This time, they chose a favorite meeting spot and stayed overnight. During the formal dinner celebration, a state legislator thanked them for their work by describing how they had changed important services to the indigent throughout the state. Then they danced!*

◆ ◆ ◆

The final milestone in our journey is an ending ritual. Refer to Ending Rituals in Appendix C (page 175) for a summary of key elements.

In meeting the last challenge of Stage 4—end the collaboration—we have learned that continuity and myth are the foundation for:

- Understanding the need for an ending.

- Creating ending rituals that include time, place, recollection of contributions, involvement of as many people as possible, inclusion of some myths, and enjoyment!

As we watch the sun set over our collaboration, we rejoice in our road, our destination, our comrades. With laughter and tears, we take off our hats and pass them to others, to those new people who have joined us and who will carry on the flag.

We sit around the campfire, here in the clearing, and tell our story. We have climbed the hills; we have slogged through the marshland; we have harvested the fertile plains; we have gathered resources for the future from the broad forest. Our gifts are many; our legacy rich.

To the best of our ability, we have built our relationships and done our work. We have achieved our desired results, and the effort has been moved into the community where it belongs. Working collaboration-to-community has endowed our effort with continuity. The stages and their challenges are complete. Now let's dance our ending!

> **"**
> *You must know the story of your culture and be proud of your ancestors*
> — *Romana Banuelos U.S. Treasurer*
> **"**

Ending Rituals

Every exit is an entrance somewhere else. These words capture well our journey together—our destination toward which we travelers move on a road of our creation. And, as we've learned, this road is really a cloverleaf—we keep coming back to the beginning, each time building on and improving what we've been doing. We don't start over. We learn, refine, shift, include others, increase the scope of our effort, and move on. Some collaborations end; others regenerate and continue. But we do not cease from our journey. And each time the road brings us back to the beginning, as weary as we may feel, we may well be ready to start all over again! ◆

> **"**
>
> *If I am not for myself, who is for me? If I am only for myself, who am I? If not now, when?*
>
> *— Rabbi Hillel First century B.C.E. sage*
>
> **"**

PART IV

How Do We End?

Let's Use These Tools

Appendix A

Twenty Factors Influencing Successful Collaborations

This handbook stems from the twenty factors influencing successful collaborations identified in *Collaboration: What Makes It Work, 2nd Edition** by Paul Mattessich, Marta Murray-Close, and Barbara Monsey of the Wilder Research Center. Grouped into six categories, this review of the research literature describes:

Factors Related to the ENVIRONMENT
1. History of collaboration or cooperation in the community
2. Collaborative group seen as a legitimate leader in the community
3. Favorable political and social climate

Factors Related to MEMBERSHIP CHARACTERISTICS
4. Mutual respect, understanding, and trust
5. Appropriate cross section of members
6. Members see collaboration as in their self-interest
7. Ability to compromise

Factors Related to PROCESS AND STRUCTURE
8. Members share a stake in both process and outcome
9. Multiple layers of participation
10. Flexibility
11. Development of clear roles and policy guidelines
12. Adaptability
13. Appropriate pace of development

Factors Related to COMMUNICATION
14. Open and frequent communication
15. Established informal and formal communication links

Factors Related to PURPOSE
16. Concrete, attainable goals and objectives
17. Shared vision
18. Unique purpose

Factors Related to RESOURCES
19. Sufficient funds, staff, material, and time
20. Skilled leadership

This research offers a base for everything we do. A collaboration inventory based on the research is available for use by your collaboration. Contact the Fieldstone Alliance for further information (800-274-6024).

* Collaboration: What Makes It Work, 2nd Edition *by Paul Mattessich, Marta Murray-Close, and Barbara Monsey is available from Fieldstone Alliance, 800-274-6024 or www.fieldstonealliance.org*

Annotated Resources

This resource list includes books, publications, and articles that have helped shape the authors' thinking and practice in collaboration. The list is by no means exhaustive. Many varied and excellent materials have been published on management, conflict resolution, planning, evaluation, promotion, and so forth. This list is for those readers who want more in-depth understanding of the concepts that shaped this book.

Appendix B

Books

Albrecht, Karl, and Ron Zemke. *Service America*. Homewood, Illinois: Dow Jones/Irwin, 1985.

Details challenges and solution for nonprofit work in the 1990s.

Angelica, Marion Peters. *Resolving Conflict in Nonprofit Organizations: The Leader's Guide to finding Constructive Solutions*. St. Paul, MN: Fieldstone Alliance, 1999.

A hands-on guide to understanding, identifying, and resolving conflice constructively in a nonprofit organization.

Atkinson, Philip. *Creating Culture Change: Key to Successful Total Quality Management*. United Kingdom: IFS Publications, 1990.

Collaboration often requires organizations to change; this book lays out the steps for making changes in the context of continuous process improvement.

Bennis, Warren. *Why Leaders Can't Lead*. San Francisco: Jossey-Bass, 1989.

Bennis explains that fragmentation of service delivery is an unconscious effort to stop change. Becoming a conscious leader of change is key to creating change on a system-wide basis.

Blake, Robert, and Jane Mouton. *Consultation*. Reading, Massachusetts: Addison-Wesley, 1976.

Strategies for helping organizations identify issues and apply solutions.

Cohen, Arthur M., and R. Douglas Smith. *The Critical Incident in Growth Groups: Theory and Technique*. San Diego: University Associates, 1976.

Looks at shaping the growth and development of groups through verbal interventions and the role of the group leader in influencing the development of a common point of view.

Gardner, John. *On Leadership*. New York: MacMillan Free Press, 1990.

Effective collaborations require effective leaders; Gardner identifies key skills for effective relationships between leaders and followers.

Gilbertsen, Beth, and Vijit Ramchandani. *The Wilder Nonprofit Field Guide to Developing Effective Teams*. St. Paul, MN: Fieldstone Alliance, 1999.

A concise guide to help a team get going, deal with predictable problems, and improve teamwork at any stage of a team's development.

Goodman, Robert. *After the Planners*. New York: Simon & Schuster, 1973.

A provocative look at the impact of changing urban systems.

Gray, Barbara. *Collaborating: Finding Common Ground for Multiparty Problems*. San Francisco: Jossey-Bass, 1989.

Describes the need for collaboration; its dynamic processes: conflict, politics, and power; various designs for collaborations; and the need to move toward a collaborative world.

Havelock, Ronald. *Change Agent's Guide to Innovation in Education*. Englewood Cliffs, NJ: Education Technology Publications, 1973.

Explains how to diagnose problems in educational institutions and intervene to create change.

Heider, John. *Tao of Leadership*. New York: Bantam Books, 1988.

Applies ancient Chinese thinking to leadership strategies for a new age.

Johnson, David, and Frank Johnson. *Joining Together*. Englewood Cliffs, NJ: Prentice Hall, 1990.

This handbook helps inexperienced group facilitators lead a series of powerful group development activities.

Kagan, Sharon L. *United We Stand: Collaboration for Child Care and Early Education Services*. New York: Teachers College Press, 1991.

Provides an excellent overview of collaboration, including its social context, rationale, and benefits, and an understanding of the collaborative process in the context of early childhood care and education.

Kanter, Rosabeth Moss. *Change Masters*. New York: Simon & Schuster, 1983.

This classic text promotes innovation in organizations.

Keirsey, David, and Marilyn Bates. *Please Understand Me*. Del Mar, California: Prometheus Nemesis, 1984.

Describes individual behavior styles according to the Myers-Briggs Inventory.

Lukas, Carol A. *Consulting with Nonprofits: A Practitioner's Guide.* St. Paul, MN: Fieldstone Alliance, 1998.

A step-by-step guide through the six stage consulting process. The book also includes information on how to run a consulting business.

McLagan, Patricia, and Peter Krembs. *On-the-Level.* St. Paul, Minnesota: McLagan International, 1988.

Action ideas for communicating about work performance that people in partnerships can use to address problems.

Pfeiffer, J. William, and John E. Jones, editors. *A Handbook of Structured Experiences for Human Relations Training, Volume V.* San Diego: University Associates, 1975.

Part of a series of handbooks of structured experiences to facilitate group beginnings, decision making, communication, leadership, team building, and so forth.

Porter, Lyman et al. *Behavior in Organizations.* New York: McGraw-Hill, 1975.

People and teams share the same kinds of problems no matter what organization they work in, but each human is a unique contributor to that group. Porter recommends many different strategies for resolving teamwork issues.

Scholtes, Peter. *Team Handbook.* Madison, WI: Joiner Publications, 1988.

An eminently usable set of exercises to build teamwork.

Senge, Peter. *Fifth Discipline.* New York: Doubleday/Currency, 1990.

Ideas for changing organizations and systems drawn from an eclectic collection of sciences.

Tannen, Deborah. *You Just Don't Understand.* New York: Ballantine, 1990.

The best intentions are not always enough for men and women to communicate successfully while solving problems. Tannen has written a volume about interpreting one another accurately.

Tjosvold, Dean, and Mary Tjosvold. *Leading the Team Organization.* New York: Lexington Books, 1991.

Building an effective team at the senior management level is critical to being a successful partner. The Tjosvolds lay out key steps for team building.

Walton, Richard. *Interpersonal Peacemaking / Third Person Consultation.* Reading, MA: Addison-Wesley Organizational Development Series, 1987.

A primer for intervening effectively in other people's conflicts.

Walton, Richard. *Managing Conflict / Interpersonal Dialogue.* Reading, MA: Addison-Wesley Organizational Development Series, 1987.

A primer for helping people resolve work-related conflicts.

Monographs and Selections

Andress, Shelby, and Eugene C. Roehlkepartain. *Working Together for Youth: A Practical Guide for Individuals and Groups.* Minneapolis, MN: Lutheran Brotherhood, 1993.

How to begin with individual motivation and move on to building a vision, taking action, and widening the circle of involvement.

Bruner, Charles. *Thinking Collaboratively: Ten Questions and Answers to Help Policy Makers Improve Children's Services.* Washington, DC: Education and Human Services Consortium, 1991.

A policy maker's guide to designing effective collaborations at state and local levels by providing an understanding of the basics of collaboration—what it is and how to know when it is working—and strategies for states and state policy makers to use.

Buhl, Alice. *Patterns of Cooperation Among Grantmakers.* Washington, DC: Council on Foundations, 1991.

Explores the process for developing joint projects, examines what funders should consider, and explains the advantages and disadvantages of current practices of collaboration.

Chynoweth, Judith K. et al. *Experiments in Systems Change: States Implement Family Policy.* Washington, DC: Council of Governors' Policy Advisors, 1992.

Discusses systems change, factors supporting the status quo and promoting systems change, and various change strategies that have been employed in nine states.

Collaboration and Conflict: Selected Readings on Collaboration. Selected Readings on Collaboration for Participants in the 1991 Annual Meeting of Independent Sector. Washington, DC: Independent Sector, 1991.

Selected readings gathered for the 1991 annual meeting of the Independent Sector on different aspects of collaboration, including understanding collaboration, patterns of collaboration, thinking collaboratively, and collaborative problem solving.

The Community Collaboration Manual. Washington, DC: National Assembly of National Health and Social Welfare Organizations, January 1991.

A manual for building collaborations with lists of items to consider.

Empowering Learners Collaborative. *Empowerment Through Collaboration: Learnings from a Literacy Collaborative.* St. Paul, MN: United Way of the Saint Paul Area, 1992.

Looks at collaboration, what it is and how it can be used, as well as the components of collaboration, the impact on the partners in the project and the learnings from the effort. An independent evaluation of the project is also available.

Himmelman, Arthur T. *Communities Working Collaboratively for a Change.* Minneapolis, MN: The Himmelman Consulting Group, (unpublished) 1991.

Presents two approaches to collaboration—betterment and empowerment—the key components and activities of each, as well as how to move from betterment to empowerment.

Mattessich, Paul W., Marta Murray-Close, and Barbara Monsey. *Collaboration: What Makes It Work, 2nd Edition.* St. Paul, MN: Fieldstone Alliance, 2001.

A review of research literature on twenty factors influencing successful collaboration. The report includes a description of each factor, implications for collaborative efforts, and illustrations from case studies.

Mattessich, Paul W. and Barbara Monsey. *Community Building: What Makes It Work.* St. Paul, MN: Fieldstone Alliance, 1997.

A review of literature that reveals twenty-eight factors influencing the success of community building initiatives. Each of the factors includes an in-depth description, examples, and practical applications, helping community builders assess their work and diagnose what's needed.

Melaville, Atelia I., and Martin J. Blank. *What It Takes: Structuring Interagency Partnerships to Connect Children and Families with Comprehensive Services.* Washington, DC: Education and Human Services Consortium, 1991.

Looks at what is needed in interagency partnerships and the state's role in local initiatives as well as the dynamics of working together, guidelines for new partners, and questions to mobilize action.

Melaville, Atelia I., Martin J. Blank, and Gelareh Asayesh. *Together We Can: A Guide for Crafting a Profamily System of Education and Human Services.* Washington, DC: U. S. Department of Education, 1993.

Discusses a vision of improved coordination of education, health, and human services for families and provides a five-stage process for achieving that vision.

Mobilization for America's Children. *Standards for Success: Building Community Supports for America's Children.* Alexandria, Virginia: United Way of America, 1993.

Provides standards for mobilization of local coalitions and programs as well as standards for tracking the well-being of children and families.

Perspectives on Collaborative Funding: A Resource for Grantmakers. Northern California Grantmakers, 1985.

A collection of twelve articles on collaborations among funders.

Articles

AtKisson, Alan. "The Innovation Diffusion Game: A Tool for Encouraging Participation in Positive Cultural Change." *In Context* No. 28, Context Institute, Bainbridge Island, Washington.

Describes nine role types usually found in the process of cultural change, and five critical characteristics of successful innovations.

Bastien, David T., and Todd J. Hostager. "Jazz as a Process of Organization Innovation." *Star Tribune*, Minneapolis, Minnesota, October 23, 1988.

An analysis of how a jazz group's ability to share information, communicate invention strategies, and coordinate complex ideas can be applied to organizations.

Berger, Renee A. "Teamworks." Speech delivered to the Minnesota Council on Foundations, September 27, 1989.

Outlines the steps for successful partnerships.

Bernard, Bonnie. "Working Together: Principles of Effective Collaboration." *Prevention Forum,* October 1989, p 4.

A selection of research-based attributes which result in effective collaborations.

Cohen, Larry, Nancy Baer, and Pam Satterwhite. "Developing Effective Coalitions: An Eight Step Guide." Contra Costa Health Services Department, Pleasant Hill, California, (unpublished) 1991.

A description of eight practical steps for creating community coalitions.

Gardner, Sid. "Failure by Fragmentation." *California Tomorrow*, Fall 1989.

Argues that funders diminish effective human services by fragmenting delivery among too many agencies, and that improvements can be made by building collaborations focused on accountability.

Hawthorne, Joyce. "Working Together for At Risk Youth." Wisconsin Department of Public Instruction, 1988.

A discussion of common barriers to coordination of services for children needing medical and social services.

Hequet, Marc. "Poof! Myth and Fable Appear as Human Development Tools." *Training*, December 1992, pp 46–50.

Discusses the emerging use of myth, fable, and archetype as workplace human development tools.

Hord, Shirley M. "A Synthesis of Research on Organizational Collaboration." *Educational Leadership*, February 1986, pp 22–26.

Distinguishes between cooperation and collaboration in the areas of beginning process, communication, resources and ownership, requirements and characteristics, leadership and control, and rewards.

Powell, Douglas R. "Evaluating Family Resource Programs: Guidelines for Appropriate Practice." Purdue University. Highlights of a keynote address from a meeting on program evaluation sponsored by the Oregon Family Resource Coalition, June 1992.

Provides five guidelines for tailoring evaluation to the unique characteristics of a family resource program.

"Public/Private Ventures: The Next Step." *The Ford Foundation Letter*, Vol. 20, No. 1, February 1989.

Two case studies of collaboration in a public-private partnership.

Ray, Karen. "Advanced Teamwork: Collaboration Among Scattered Teams." Karen Ray Associates, Minneapolis, Minnesota, (unpublished) 1991.

Describes four major tasks of working closely together while separated by distance.

Sabatino, Frank. "How Collaboration Is Influencing Boards' Strategic Plans." *Trustee*, August, 1992, pp 8–10.

Looks at the community forces that are pushing hospitals to consider collaboration: resources, ethics, cost control, physician input, business input, and chief executive officer accountability. ◆

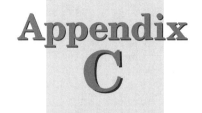

Appendix C

Documentation Forms/Worksheets

Many times in a collaboration, documentation is the only proof we have that we have been accomplishing important work. The following forms, guides, and checklists help document what our collaboration is doing.

Copy the ones here and use them freely and liberally in order to:

1. Keep track of progress, both successes and learnings

2. Update inactive collaboration members

3. Plan and organize work (one funder used these forms to contract with a group about what tasks would be completed in what order)

4. Report accomplishments to supervisors, officials, and funders

5. Update records regularly

6. Create a history for orienting new members

7. Tell stories to help convince the greater community that collaboration can change systems

8. Celebrate all that's been achieved

Electronic versions of these worksheets may be downloaded from the publisher's web site. Use the following URL to obtain the worksheets:

http://www.fieldstonealliance.org/worksheets

Access code: W032cHc94

These online worksheets are intended for use in the same way as photocopies of the worksheets, but they are in a form that allows you to type in your responses and reformat the worksheets to fit your collaboration. Please do not download the worksheets unless you or your organization has purchased this workbook.

As of *(date)* _____   Page ____ of ____

List the organizations involved and their representatives. Initial self-interests and possible contributions can be declared by individual/organization or summarized for all involved. How these factors are listed depends on the level of trust—the higher the trust, the more individuals can lay claim to their declarations. Update this roster regularly.

Organization *Representative's name, phone number, organization name and address, and type of organization (i.e. nonprofit, government, grassroots, funder, and so forth)*	**Initial Self-Interests** *Organizational and Personal Gains*	**Possible Contributions** *Powers and Commitments*

Copyright © 1994 Fieldstone Alliance, www.fieldstonealliance.org

Continued

Membership Roster   Document 1A

As of *(date)* _____   Page _____ of _____

Organization *Representative's name, phone number, organization name and address, and type of organization (i.e. nonprofit, government, grassroots, funder, and so forth)*	Initial Self-Interests *Organizational and Personal Gains*	Possible Contributions *Powers and Commitments*

Copyright © 1994 Fieldstone Alliance, www.fieldstonealliance.org

Calling the Next Meeting   (send to participants in advance of next meeting)

Collaboration name or purpose:

Purpose of next meeting:

Meeting date:

Location:

Start and end times:

Convener: **Phone:**

Participants (see membership roster for addresses and phone numbers):

Action Agenda

Item	Disposition *For information, discussion, or decision*	Responsibility	Time

Copyright © 1994 Fieldstone Alliance, www.fieldstonealliance.org

Continued

Summary of Decisions Made/Actions to be Taken

This summarizes the previous meeting and accompanies the agendas for the next meeting.

Decision Made/Action to be Taken	Responsibility	Deadline

Summary of Achievements to Date

This is a log of all achievements. It provides an excellent history and basis for evaluation. Update it regularly.

Achievements	Responsibility	Date

Copyright © 1994 Fieldstone Alliance, www.fieldstonealliance.org

COMMON MISSION- educate + teach life skills to our youth in order to help them live strong productive life.

This document provides an excellent record of the rationale for the vision and focus statements. It also aids in achieving support from key stakeholders.

1. What is our destination—what will we achieve, for whom and where?

To help children deal with situations - whether it is homelessness, abuse, diabetes (made fun of -) discrimination or embarrassment for being different

live skills that will help.

strength + respect for self body

2. What is the scope of our effort—how big, how many, how much?

What valueable service or product would ea group provide for health or well being of community -

3. How is this destination unique among members of the collaboration?

4. How can we phrase the vision statement so that it is not complicated?
Our draft vision is:

5. After considering our statement, how can we rephrase it so that it is easy to understand and easy to repeat?

> **Our vision is:**

6. Imagining that we have fifteen seconds to communicate the essence of our vision, what short phrase best captures the heart of it?

> **Our focus is:**

Copyright © 1994 Fieldstone Alliance, www.fieldstonealliance.org

Before we proceed with this step, we need to make sure that we have accomplished the following:

- **Declared Self-Interests**
  Attach or note the location of Document 1A—an updated membership roster including member's personal and organizational self-interests.

- **Recorded Achievements to Date**
  Attach or note the location of Document 1B—meeting summaries and record of achievements. Continually accumulate records of achievements.

- **Identified Our Vision and Focus Statements**
  Attach or note the location of Document 1C.

We're now ready to develop statements of our desired results and strategies.

Communal Benefits

Outline what we are trying to achieve.

What are our long-term desired results?

What are our short-term desired results?

Are the results we've identified tangible? Can we measure them? Can others recognize them?

Copyright © 1994 Fieldstone Alliance, www.fieldstonealliance.org

Key Strategies   Give the key stakeholders perspectives; rate them "for," "against," or "persuadable." Sequence the approach—who talks to whom, and in what order.

Key Stakeholder	Perspective	Rate (F/A/P)	Sequence

Redefined Results   Now we restate our desired results integrating stakeholders' perspectives.

Redefined long-term results:

Redefined short-term results:

Strategic Aim   List specific actions to influence stakeholders.

Decision Made/Action to be Taken	Responsibility	Deadline

Copyright © 1994 Fieldstone Alliance, www.fieldstonealliance.org

Obtain a letter of commitment from each participating organization. Ask that the letter be on the organization's letterhead and be signed by highest authority possible. Check off the following to make sure they are included:

- ❏ Commitment to planning and an understanding that the process takes time

- ❏ Acknowledgment of the other partners and their contributions

- ❏ Commitment to the vision, focus, desired results, and strategies that have been laid out

- ❏ Statement of what the organization expects in return for participation

- ❏ Listing of the types of powers that can be committed (connections, expertise, funds, and so forth)

- ❏ Areas of authority where the representative can commit resources and act on behalf of the organization

Copyright © 1994 Fieldstone Alliance, www.fieldstonealliance.org

A record of conflict is valuable to show that progress has been made, to revisit resolutions should similar issues arise again, to evaluate accomplishments, and to keep as an historical record. Attach conflicts and their resolutions to meeting summaries or keep them with other milestone documents. Include at least the following in the record:

Date	Type of Conflict	Facilitator and Process Used	Resolutions	Healing Rituals

Copyright © 1994 Fieldstone Alliance, www.fieldstonealliance.org

Continued

Date	Type of Conflict	Facilitator and Process Used	Resolutions	Healing Rituals

Copyright © 1994 Fieldstone Alliance, www.fieldstonealliance.org

Determine how to organize to get work done efficiently. Ask: "What kinds of groups do we need to form in order to do our work? Is it critical for all of us to make all decisions, or can some decisions be made by subgroups? How much must we communicate with one another?"

1. **Structure.** Sketch the collaboration's structure—table, wheel, or other (see page 82 for more information):

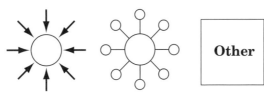

2. **Level of Authority.** Decide if authority is hierarchical, individual-based, group centered, or other. Sketch how members relate to each other (see page 83 for more information):

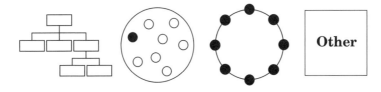

3. **Roles.** Assign specific responsibilities to individuals, small groups, the whole group, and/or staff. Add those responsibilities to the sketch of levels of authority above.

Copyright © 1994 Fieldstone Alliance, www.fieldstonealliance.org   *Continued*

4. **Resources.** Decide what is needed; what will be the source (members, the community, in-kind funding); and who will control which resources:

Resources Needed	Source	Who Controls

Copyright © 1994 Fieldstone Alliance, www.fieldstonealliance.org

Update this form regularly for all decisions made by the collaboration.

Decisions to be Made *About collaboration process and results*	With What Level of Authority *Unilateral, consultative, consensual, democratic, or delegated*	Who Makes Them	Where that Person Fits in the Structure

Copyright © 1994 Fieldstone Alliance, www.fieldstonealliance.org

Note communications, who receives them, and how.

Type of Communication/Information/Reward	Who It Goes To	By What Means

Copyright © 1994 Fieldstone Alliance, www.fieldstonealliance.org

Briefly restate the desired results and strategies (with revisions as needed):

Complete the following action implementation plan:

Actions to Be Taken	Who is Responsible	By When	With What Accountability	Cost

Copyright © 1994 Fieldstone Alliance, www.fieldstonealliance.org

Continued

Action Implementation Plan   Document 3A

Actions to Be Taken	Who is Responsible	By When	With What Accountability	Cost
Note what information will be shared with whom and who is responsible for doing so. Add this to the communications plan—Document 2D.			Total Cost:	

Copyright © 1994 Fieldstone Alliance, www.fieldstonealliance.org

Use this checklist to create the joint agreements between organizations:

❏ What **degree of closeness** have all organizations agreed on for the joint agreements? (Interagency committee, single point, lead agency, consolidation, incorporation)

❏ What **authority** will each organization exercise?

❏ Which **responsibilities** will each organization fulfill?

Copyright © 1994 Fieldstone Alliance, www.fieldstonealliance.org

Continued

❏ What kinds of **powers and other resources** will each organization contribute?

❏ Which **key people** in each organization must sign the agreement and have they signed?

❏ What important **policies, procedures, and operations** have to be changed in each organization to further the collaboration, and what is the plan for implementing those changes?

❏ Who has responsibility for **drafting the agreements** and negotiating any differences among the member organizations?

Copyright © 1994 Fieldstone Alliance, www.fieldstonealliance.org

Review all milestones to date, including the meeting summaries. Then, make sure to cover the following:

Process Evaluation	Results Evaluation
1. State the separate self-interests of each organization and how it will know when its self-interests are being met:	1. State the desired community benefits (for example, reduction in homelessness) and how the collaboration will know if the effort is successful:
2. Note when milestones are accomplished and what helped and hindered their accomplishment:	2. Outline the methods being used, such as lobbying, delivery of services, creation of information packets:
3. Describe communicative processes between members of the collaboration:	3. Summarize critical junctures toward achieving communal benefits:

Copyright © 1994 Fieldstone Alliance, www.fieldstonealliance.org

Continued

Process Evaluation	Results Evaluation
4. Summarize the collaboration's impact on the member organizations. What has each contributed? How did the collaboration change the way each organization does business?	4. Describe the characteristics of the community being targeted, the number and diversity of people involved, their reaction to the effort and its methods, and changes in the community that might be attributed to this effort:
5. Note side effects. Who else becomes involved? How does that help the effort?	5. Note side effects. Who else becomes involved? How does that help the effort?
6. Other:	6. Other:

Now draw some conclusions:

- What lessons have we learned?

- What do we need to change or add?

- What previous challenges should we review?

Copyright © 1994 Fieldstone Alliance, www.fieldstonealliance.org

To ensure that our collaboration remains adaptable and flexible, we need to stop to review at least the following:

❏ What is changing among member organizations, in the community, and in social, political, and economic trends (adaptability)?

❏ What is changing in the collaboration itself (flexibility)?

❏ What do we need to change to be more adaptable and flexible?

❏ Who has finished their work for the collaboration?

❏ How should we ask them to leave?

Copyright © 1994 Fieldstone Alliance, www.fieldstonealliance.org

Continued

❏ Who else needs to be involved to further the effort. In other words, what powers and preferences are needed now?

❏ How should we approach new members?

❏ How should we orient and integrate them?

❏ What is the best structure for the reformed collaboration?

❏ How will we celebrate what we have accomplished and the people who have made those contributions?

Copyright © 1994 Fieldstone Alliance, www.fieldstonealliance.org

1. **First we ask ourselves:**

   - What myths can we tell about the results we have achieved?

   - What myths can we tell about how the collaboration began and evolved?

   - What images (rather than explanations) do we want to convey about what we've done and who we are?

   - What symbols can we use to convey those images and tell our stories?

2. **Next we draft an image statement and review it with others to determine its impact:**

3. **Then we refine the statement.**

   Our image is:

Copyright © 1994 Fieldstone Alliance, www.fieldstonealliance.org

Continued

4. Last, we lay out our promotion campaign:

- What is our message?

- What specific next steps are we asking our publics to take?

- How will we promote the message?

- What specific steps will we undertake?

- Who will be responsible for which steps?

- What will it cost?

- Where will we obtain the resources?

- When will we finish each step?

Copyright © 1994 Fieldstone Alliance, www.fieldstonealliance.org

In planning how to involve the community in our collaborative effort, we need to consider the following:

❏ What do we need to tell the public about collaboration so that we attract future leaders?

❏ Who are potential representatives of diverse community interests?

❏ How do we adjust our decision-making process to make it more open and accessible?

❏ What programs and policies do we need to change because they are outmoded?

❏ How can we increase our base of support to work more widely in the community?

Copyright © 1994 Fieldstone Alliance, www.fieldstonealliance.org

Continued

❏ How can member organizations enhance their internal leadership?

❏ How will key stakeholders in the community at large be influenced?

❏ Who are the potential leaders?

❏ How will we select, charge, and train them?

❏ How will present leaders let go of the reins?

❏ What kinds of forums can we build in the community that generate wide ownership, invite discussion, and challenge assumptions?

Copyright © 1994 Fieldstone Alliance, www.fieldstonealliance.org

To begin to change systems, we need to answer the following questions:

1. **What are present conditions?** Because extensive data exists in most communities, you may have little need to gather more information.

2. **How do people address those conditions?** Bring in the perspectives of all fields: arts, human services, environment, health care, education, media, and business; and of all sectors: public, private, and nonprofit.

3. **What is our picture of desired results?** Remember the desired picture is one of structural change, not of providing more programs to alleviate problems.

4. **How do we map out all the interrelated parts of the system and how they are linked?** In relation to the desired results, describe the impetus for and the blocks to change in each part of the system.

5. **What are the leverage points in the system?** Leverage points are those places to which you can apply pressure that will move the impetus for change forward and/or reduce the blocks to change. The exertion of leverage needs to have the greatest return for energy expended, so focus on those most likely to move. Often the leverage points are key individuals and organizations, but sometimes there is a community-wide perspective that must be addressed.

6. **How do we redefine the desired results from the viewpoints of the various leverage points?** Language is crucial for increasing the impetus for change or reducing the blocks to change.

Copyright © 1994 Fieldstone Alliance, www.fieldstonealliance.org

Continued

7. **What action can we take, at the smallest level, to begin change?** Individuals and small groups are easier to influence than government or multinational corporations. Use the aggregated achievements in smaller arenas to influence larger parts of the system.

8. **What multi-faceted approaches can we use in all fields and sectors?** Although many approaches must be done in concert with each other, some can be implemented sequentially.

9. **How do we help parts of the system form new relationships?** These relationships are to be with other parts of the system and with other systems which had no earlier relationships.

10. **When will we stop and learn?** Extract and apply the learnings to other similar situations which in turn produce new learnings.

Copyright © 1994 Fieldstone Alliance, www.fieldstonealliance.org

In planning ending rituals, fill in the circles and build each element into the celebration:

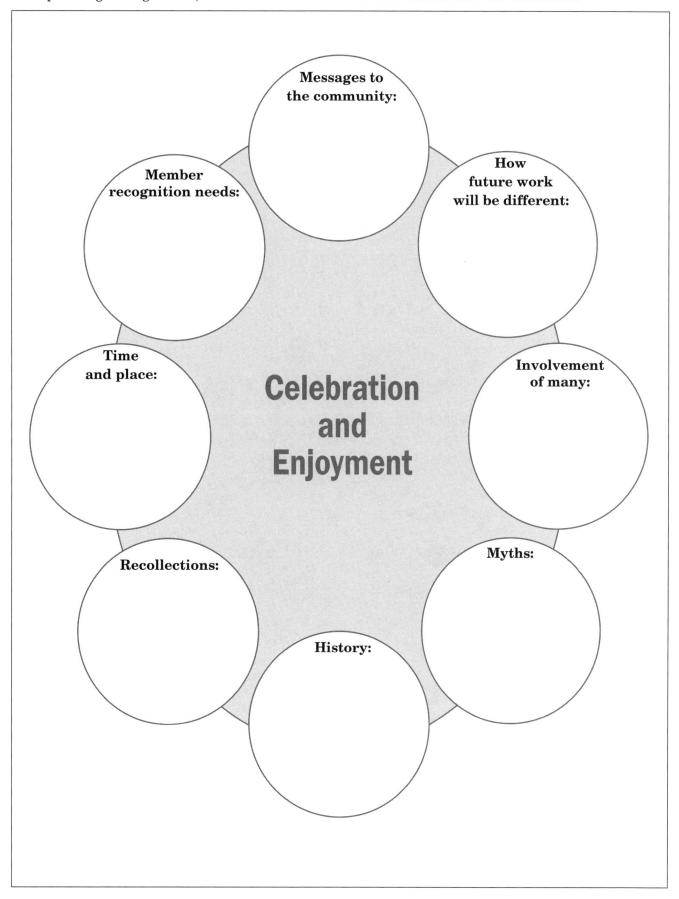

Copyright © 1994 Fieldstone Alliance, www.fieldstonealliance.org

More results-oriented books from Fieldstone Alliance

Collaboration

Collaboration Handbook
Creating, Sustaining, and Enjoying the Journey
by Michael Winer and Karen Ray

Shows you how to get a collaboration going, set goals, determine everyone's roles, create an action plan, and evaluate the results. Includes a case study of one collaboration from start to finish, helpful tips on how to avoid pitfalls, and worksheets to keep everyone on track.

192 pages, softcover   Item # 069032

Collaboration: What Makes It Work, 2nd Ed.
by Paul Mattessich, PhD, Marta Murray-Close, BA, and Barbara Monsey, MPH

An in-depth review of current collaboration research. Major findings are summarized, critical conclusions are drawn, and twenty key factors influencing successful collaborations are identified. Includes The Wilder Collaboration Factors Inventory, which groups can use to assess their collaboration.

104 pages, softcover   Item # 069326

The Nimble Collaboration
Fine-Tuning Your Collaboration for Lasting Success
by Karen Ray

Shows you ways to make your existing collaboration more responsive, flexible, and productive. Provides three key strategies to help your collaboration respond quickly to changing environments and participants.

136 pages, softcover   Item # 069288

Community Building

Community Building: What Makes It Work
by Wilder Research Center

Reveals twenty-eight keys to help you build community more effectively. Includes detailed descriptions of each factor, case examples of how they play out, and practical questions to assess your work.

112 pages, softcover   Item # 069121

Community Economic Development Handbook
by Mihailo Temali

A concrete, practical handbook to turning any neighborhood around. It explains how to start a community economic development organization, and then lays out the steps of four proven and powerful strategies for revitalizing inner-city neighborhoods.

288 pages, softcover   Item # 069369

The Wilder Nonprofit Field Guide to
Conducting Community Forums
by Carol Lukas and Linda Hoskins

Provides step-by-step instruction to plan and carry out exciting, successful community forums that will educate the public, build consensus, focus action, or influence policy.

128 pages, softcover   Item # 069318

Lobbying & Advocacy

The Lobbying and Advocacy Handbook for Nonprofit Organizations
Shaping Public Policy at the State and Local Level
by Marcia Avner

The Lobbying and Advocacy Handbook is a planning guide and resource for nonprofit organizations that want to influence issues that matter to them. This book will help you decide whether to lobby and then put plans in place to make it work.

240 pages, softcover   Item # 069261

The Nonprofit Board Member's Guide to Lobbying and Advocacy
by Marcia Avner

Written specifically for board members, this guide helps organizations increase their impact on policy decisions. It reveals how board members can be involved in planning for and implementing successful lobbying efforts.

96 pages, softcover   Item # 069393

Finance

Bookkeeping Basics
What Every Nonprofit Bookkeeper Needs to Know
by Debra L. Ruegg and Lisa M. Venkatrathnam

Complete with step-by-step instructions, a glossary of accounting terms, detailed examples, and handy reproducible forms, this book will enable you to successfully meet the basic bookkeeping requirements of your nonprofit organization— even if you have little or no formal accounting training.

128 pages, softcover   Item # 069296

Coping with Cutbacks
The Nonprofit Guide to Success When Times Are Tight
by Emil Angelica and Vincent Hyman

Shows you practical ways to involve business, government, and other nonprofits to solve problems together. Also includes 185 cutback strategies you can put to use right away.

128 pages, softcover   Item # 069091

Financial Leadership for Nonprofit Executives
Guiding Your Organization to Long-term Success
by Jeanne Peters and Elizabeth Schaffer

Provides nonprofit leaders with a practical guide to protecting and growing the assets of their organizations and with accomplishing as much mission as possible with those resources.

144 pages, softcover   Item # 06944X

Venture Forth! The Essential Guide to Starting a Moneymaking Business in Your Nonprofit Organization
by Rolfe Larson

The most complete guide on nonprofit business development. Building on the experience of dozens of organizations, this handbook gives you a time-tested approach for finding, testing, and launching a successful nonprofit business venture.

272 pages, softcover   Item # 069245

Management & Leadership

Benchmarking for Nonprofits
How to Measure, Manage, and Improve Results
by Jason Saul

This book defines a formal, systematic, and reliable way to benchmark (the onging process of measuring your organization against leaders) from preparing your organization to measuring performance and implementing best practices.

128 pages, softcover   Item # 069431

Consulting with Nonprofits: A Practitioner's Guide
by Carol A. Lukas

A step-by-step, comprehensive guide for consultants. Addresses the art of consulting, how to run your business, and much more. Also includes tips and anecdotes from thirty skilled consultants.

240 pages, softcover   Item # 069172

The Wilder Nonprofit Field Guide to Crafting Effective Mission and Vision Statements
by Emil Angelica

Guides you through two six-step processes that result in a mission statement, vision statement, or both. Shows how a clarified mission and vision lead to more effective leadership, decisions, fundraising, and management.

88 pages, softcover   Item # 06927X

The Wilder Nonprofit Field Guide to Developing Effective Teams
by Beth Gilbertsen and Vijit Ramchandani

Helps you understand, start, and maintain a team. Provides tools and techniques for writing a mission statement, setting goals, conducting effective meetings, creating ground rules to manage team dynamics, making decisions in teams, creating project plans, and developing team spirit.

80 pages, softcover   Item # 069202

The Five Life Stages of Nonprofit Organizations
Where You Are, Where You're Going, and What to Expect When You Get There
by Judith Sharken Simon with J. Terence Donovan

Shows you what's "normal" for each development stage which helps you plan for transitions, stay on track, and avoid unnecessary struggles. This guide also includes The Wilder Nonprofit Life Stage Assessment to plot and understand your organization's progress in seven arenas of organization development.

128 pages, softcover   Item # 069229

The Manager's Guide to Program Evaluation:
Planning, Contracting, and Managing for Useful Results
by Paul W. Mattessich, PhD

Explains how to plan and manage an evaluation that will help identify your organization's successes, share information with key audiences, and improve services.

96 pages, softcover   Item # 069385

The Nonprofit Mergers Workbook
The Leader's Guide to Considering, Negotiating, and Executing a Merger
by David La Piana

A merger can be a daunting and complex process. Save time, money, and untold frustration with this highly practical guide that makes the process manageable and controllable. Includes case studies, decision trees, twenty-two worksheets, checklists, tips, and complete step-by-step guidance from seeking partners to writing the merger agreement, and more.

240 pages, softcover   Item # 069210

The Nonprofit Mergers Workbook Part II
Unifying the Organization after a Merger
by La Piana Associates

Once the merger agreement is signed, the question becomes: How do we make this merger work? *Part II* helps you create a comprehensive plan to achieve *integration*—bringing together people, programs, processes, and systems from two (or more) organizations into a single, unified whole.

248 pages, includes CD-ROM   Item # 069415

Nonprofit Stewardship
A Better Way to Lead Your Mission-Based Organization
by Peter C. Brinckerhoff

You may lead a not-for-profit organization, but it's not your organization. It belongs to the community it serves. You are the steward—the manager of resources that belong to someone else. The stewardship model of leadership can help your organization improve its mission capability by forcing you to keep your organization's mission foremost. It helps you make decisions that are best for the people your organization serves. In other words, stewardship helps you do more good for more people.

272 pages, softcover   Item # 069423

For current prices or to order visit us online at 🖥 **www.fieldstonealliance.org**

Resolving Conflict in Nonprofit Organizations
The Leader's Guide to Finding Constructive Solutions
by Marion Peters Angelica

Helps you identify conflict, decide whether to intervene, un-cover and deal with the true issues, and design and conduct a conflict resolution process. Includes exercises to learn and practice conflict resolution skills, guidance on handling unique conflicts such as harassment and discrimination, and when (and where) to seek outside help with litigation, arbitration, and mediation.

192 pages, softcover   *Item # 069164*

Strategic Planning Workbook for Nonprofit Organizations, Revised and Updated
by Bryan Barry

Chart a wise course for your nonprofit's future. This time-tested workbook gives you practical step-by-step guidance, real-life examples, one nonprofit's complete strategic plan, and easy-to-use worksheets.

144 pages, softcover   *Item # 069075*

Marketing & Fundraising

The Wilder Nonprofit Field Guide to
Conducting Successful Focus Groups
by Judith Sharken Simon

Shows how to collect valuable information without a lot of money or special expertise. Using this proven technique, you'll get essential opinions and feedback to help you check out your assumptions, do better strategic planning, improve services or products, and more.

80 pages, softcover   *Item # 069199*

The Wilder Nonprofit Field Guide to
Fundraising on the Internet
by Gary M. Grobman, Gary B. Grant, and Steve Roller

Your quick road map to using the Internet for fundraising. Shows you how to attract new donors, troll for grants, get listed on sites that assist donors, and learn more about the art of fundraising. Includes detailed reviews of 77 web sites use-ful to fundraisers, including foundations, charities, prospect research sites, and sites that assist donors.

64 pages, softcover   *Item # 069180*

Marketing Workbook for Nonprofit Organizations
Volume I: Develop the Plan
by Gary J. Stern

Don't just wish for results—get them! Here's how to create a straightforward, usable marketing plan. Includes the six Ps of Marketing, how to use them effectively, a sample marketing plan, tips on using the Internet, and worksheets.

208 pages, softcover   *Item # 069253*

Marketing Workbook for Nonprofit Organizations Volume II: Mobilize People for Marketing Success
by Gary J. Stern

Put together a successful promotional campaign based on the most persuasive tool of all: personal contact. Learn how to mobilize your entire organization, its staff, volunteers, and sup-porters in a focused, one-to-one marketing campaign. Comes with *Pocket Guide for Marketing Representatives*. In it, your marketing representatives can record key campaign messages and find motivational reminders.

192 pages, softcover   *Item # 069105*

Board Tools

The Best of the Board Café
Hands-on Solutions for Nonprofit Boards
by Jan Masaoka, CompassPoint Nonprofit Services

Gathers the most requested articles from the e-newsletter, *Board Café*. You'll find a lively menu of ideas, information, opinions, news, and resources to help board members give and get the most out of their board service.

232 pages, softcover   *Item # 069407*

The Nonprofit Board Member's Guide to
Lobbying and Advocacy
by Marcia Avner

96 pages, softcover   *Item # 069393*

Keeping the Peace
by Marion Angelica

Written especially for board members and chief executives, this book is a step-by-step guide to ensure that everyone is treated fairly adn a feasible solution is reached.

48 pages, softcover   *Item # 860127*

Funder's Guides

Community Visions, Community Solutions
Grantmaking for Comprehensive Impact
by Joseph A. Connor and Stephanie Kadel-Taras

Helps foundations, community funds, government agencies, and other grantmakers uncover a community's highest aspira-tion for itself, and support and sustain strategic efforts to get to workable solutions.

128 pages, softcover   *Item # 06930X*

Strengthening Nonprofit Performance
A Funder's Guide to Capacity Building
by Paul Connolly and Carol Lukas

This practical guide synthesizes the most recent capacity building practice and research into a collection of strategies, steps, and examples that you can use to get started on or im-prove funding to strengthen nonprofit organizations.

176 pages, softcover   *Item # 069377*

Violence Prevention & Intervention

The Little Book of Peace
Designed and illustrated by Kelly O. Finnerty

A pocket-size guide to help people think about violence and talk about it with their families and friends. You may download a free copy of *The Little Book of Peace* from our web site at www.wilder.org/pubs.

24 pages (minimum order 10 copies)   Item # 069083
*Also available in **Spanish** and **Hmong** language editions.*

Journey Beyond Abuse: A Step-by-Step Guide to Facilitating Women's Domestic Abuse Groups
by Kay-Laurel Fischer, MA, LP, and Michael F. McGrane, LICSW

Create a program where women increase their understanding of the dynamics of abuse, feel less alone and isolated, and have a greater awareness of channels to safety. Includes twenty-one group activities that you can combine to create groups of differing length and focus.

208 pages, softcover   Item # 069148

Moving Beyond Abuse: Stories and Questions for Women Who Have Lived with Abuse
(Companion guided journal to *Journey Beyond Abuse*)

A series of stories and questions that can be used in coordination with the sessions provided in the facilitator's guide or with the guidance of a counselor in other forms of support.

88 pages, softcover   Item # 069156

Foundations for Violence-Free Living:
A Step-by-Step Guide to Facilitating Men's Domestic Abuse Groups
by David J. Mathews, MA, LICSW

A complete guide to facilitating a men's domestic abuse program. Includes twenty-nine activities, detailed guidelines for presenting each activity, and a discussion of psychological issues that may arise out of each activity.

240 pages, softcover   Item # 069059

On the Level
(Participant's workbook to *Foundations for Violence-Free Living*)
Contains forty-nine worksheets including midterm and final evaluations. Men can record their progress.

160 pages, softcover   Item # 069067

What Works in Preventing Rural Violence
by Wilder Research Center

An in-depth review of eighty-eight effective strategies you can use to prevent and intervene in violent behaviors, improve services for victims, and reduce repeat offenses. This report also includes a Community Report Card with step-by-step directions on how you can collect, record, and use information about violence in your community.

94 pages, softcover   Item # 069040

ORDERING INFORMATION

Order online, or by phone or fax

 Online: www.fieldstonealliance.org
E-mail: books@fieldstonealliance.org

 Call toll-free: 800-274-6024

 Mail: Fieldstone Alliance
Attn: Publishing
60 Plato Boulevard East, Suite 150
Saint Paul, MN 55107

Our NO-RISK guarantee

If you aren't completely satisfied with any book for any reason, simply send it back within 30 days for a full refund.

Pricing and discounts

For current prices and discounts, please visit our web site at www.fieldstonealliance.org or call toll free at 800-274-6024.

Do you have a book idea?

Fieldstone Alliance seeks manuscripts and proposals for books in the fields of nonprofit management and community development. To get a copy of our author guidelines, please call us at 800-274-6024. You can also download them from our web site at www.fieldstonealliance.org.

Visit us online

You'll find information about Fieldstone Alliance and more details on our books, such as table of contents, pricing, discounts, endorsements, and more, at www.fieldstonealliance.org.

Quality assurance

We strive to make sure that all the books we publish are helpful and easy to use. Our major workbooks are tested and critiqued by experts before being published. Their comments help shape the final book and—we trust—make it more useful to you.